ASPECTS OF BRITISH MUSIC OF THE 1990s

Aspects of British Music
of the 1990s

Edited by

PETER O'HAGAN

ASHGATE

Published by
Ashgate Publishing Limited
Gower House
Croft Road
Aldershot
Hants GU11 3HR
England

Ashgate Publishing Company
Suite 420
101 Cherry Street
Burlington
VT 05401-4405
USA

Ashgate website: http://www.ashgate.com

British Library Cataloguing in Publication Data
Aspects of British music of the 1990s
    1. Music - Great Britain - 20th century - History and criticism - Congresses
    2. Composers - Great Britain - Congresses   3. Composers - Great Britain - Interviews
    I. O'Hagan, Peter
    780.9 2241' 09049

Library of Congress Cataloging-in-Publication Data
Aspects of British music of the 1990s / edited by Peter O'Hagan. -- 1st ed.
      p. cm.
    Papers from an unnamed conference held in 1999 at the University of Surrey,
    Roehampton. Includes bibliographical references (p.).
    ISBN 0-7546-3041-2 (alk. paper)
      1. Music--Great Britain--20th century--Congresses. I. O'Hagan, Peter.

  ML285.5 .A86 2002
  780' .941' 0904--dc21

                                2002024922

ISBN 0 7546 3041 2

Typeset in 10/12pt Times New Roman by Q3 Bookwork, Loughborough, Leicestershire
and printed in Great Britain by MPG Books Ltd., Bodmin, Cornwall.

Contents

List of Figures   vii

List of Illustrations   viii

List of Music Examples   ix

Notes on Contributors   xii

Acknowledgements   xiv

Introduction   xv
Peter O'Hagan

PART I: ESSAYS   1

1   James Dillon, Thomas Adès, and the Pleasures of Allusion   3
     Arnold Whittall

2   Multiple Choice? Composing and Climate Change in the 1990s   29
     Julian Johnson

3   The Artists' Dilemma   39
     Edwin Roxburgh

4   In the Shadows of Song: Birtwistle's Nine Movements for String Quartet   47
     Robert Adlington

5   Precarious Rapture: The Recent Music of Jonathan Harvey   63
     Julian Johnson

6   Perception of Structure: *Sonata-Rondo* for Piano (1996)   85
     Sebastian Forbes

PART II: INTERVIEWS   109

7   A Conversation with Harrison Birtwistle   111
     Robert Adlington

8   An Interview with Jonathan Harvey   119
     Julian Johnson

9   A Conversation with James Dillon   131
     Keith Potter

Contents

10   An Interview with Edwin Roxburgh   141
     Caroline Potter

11   A Conversation with Sebastian Forbes   149
     Ateş Orga

Index   161

List of Figures

4.1   *Pulse Shadows*   47

4.2   Nine Movements for String Quartet   49

4.3   Todesfuge – Frieze 4: resulting structure   61

6.1   Overall plan   100

List of Illustrations

1   Thomas Adès © Maurice Foxall   4

2   Harrison Birtwistle. Photo by Richard Kalina   112

3   Jonathan Harvey © Maurice Foxall   120

4   James Dillon. Photo by Dylan Collard   132

5   Edwin Roxburgh. Author's collection   142

6   Sebastian Forbes. Author's collection   150

List of Music Examples

1.1   James Dillon, Third String Quartet, 3rd movement from bar 30   8
        From Edition Peters No. 7522 © 1998 by Hinrichsen Edition,
        Peters Edition, London. Reproduced by kind permission of the
        publishers
1.2   James Dillon, Third String Quartet, 3rd movement, ending   10
        From Edition Peters No. 7522 © 1998 by Hinrichsen Edition,
        Peters Edition, London. Reproduced by kind permission of the
        publishers
1.3   James Dillon, Third String Quartet, 1st movement, opening   12
        From Edition Peters No. 7522 © 1998 by Hinrichsen Edition,
        Peters Edition, London. Reproduced by kind permission of the
        publishers
1.4   James Dillon, Third String Quartet, 1st movement from bar 54   13
        From Edition Peters No. 7522 © 1998 by Hinrichsen Edition,
        Peters Edition, London. Reproduced by kind permission of the
        publishers
1.5(a) James Dillon, Third String Quartet, 2nd movement, opening   15
        From Edition Peters No. 7522 © 1998 by Hinrichsen Edition,
        Peters Edition, London. Reproduced by kind permission of the
        publishers
1.5(b) James Dillon, Third String Quartet, 2nd movement, ending   16
        From Edition Peters No. 7522 © 1998 by Hinrichsen Edition,
        Peters Edition, London. Reproduced by kind permission
        of the publishers
1.6   Thomas Adès, *Arcadiana*, 4th movement, opening   17
        © 1995 by Faber Music Ltd. Reproduced by kind permission
        of the publishers
1.7   Thomas Adès, *Arcadiana*, 6th movement, opening   18
        © 1995 by Faber Music Ltd. Reproduced by kind permission
        of the publishers
1.8   Thomas Adès, *Arcadiana*, 6th movement (motivic elements)   20
1.9   Thomas Adès, *Arcadiana*, 6th movement (hypothetical Elgarian
        model)   21
1.10(a) Thomas Adès, *Arcadiana*, 1st movement, bars 1–3 and 9–11   23
        © 1995 by Faber Music Ltd. Reproduced by kind permission
        of the publishers

1.10(b) Thomas Adès, *Arcadiana*, 7th movement, bars 1–3 © 1995 by   24
          Faber Music Ltd. Reproduced by kind permission of the publishers
4.1   Harrison Birtwistle, characteristic texture of second half of
          Fantasias 1 and 2   53
          © Copyright 1996 by Boosey & Hawkes Music Publishers Ltd
          and Universal Edition (London) Ltd. Reproduced by permission
          of Boosey & Hawkes Music Publishers Ltd
4.2   Harrison Birtwistle, characteristic rhythmic idea in Fantasias 3,
          4 and 5   55
          © Copyright 1996 by Boosey & Hawkes Music Publishers Ltd
          and Universal Edition (London) Ltd. Reproduced by permission
          of Boosey & Hawkes Music Publishers Ltd
4.3   Harrison Birtwistle, 'tuning up' music in Fantasia 4   57
          © Copyright 1996 by Boosey & Hawkes Music Publishers Ltd
          and Universal Edition (London) Ltd. Reproduced by permission
          of Boosey & Hawkes Music Publishers Ltd
4.4   Harrison Birtwistle, repeated motives in Frieze 3   58
          © Copyright 1996 by Boosey & Hawkes Music Publishers Ltd
          and Universal Edition (London) Ltd. Reproduced by permission
          of Boosey & Hawkes Music Publishers Ltd
4.5   Harrison Birtwistle, five-part subject from Todesfuge–Frieze 4   60
          © Copyright 1996 by Boosey & Hawkes Music Publishers Ltd
          and Universal Edition (London) Ltd. Reproduced by permission
          of Boosey & Hawkes Music Publishers Ltd
5.1   Jonathan Harvey, Percussion Concerto, 1st movement, J to M
          (16 bars)   66
          © 1997 Faber Music Ltd. Reproduced by permission of the
          publishers
5.2   Jonathan Harvey, String Quartet no. 3, opening, pp. 1–2 (bars 1–5) 70
          © 1995 Faber Music Ltd. Reproduced by permission of the
          publishers
5.3   Jonathan Harvey, *Advaya*, pp. 8–9   74
          © 1994 Faber Music Ltd. Reproduced by permission of the
          publishers
5.4   Jonathan Harvey, *Soleil Noir/Chitra*, pp. 45–8, BB to DD (12 bars) 77
          © 1995 Faber Music Ltd. Reproduced by permission of the
          publishers
5.5   Jonathan Harvey, *Calling Across Time*, pp. 3–5, B to D (13 bars)   81
          © 1998 Faber Music Ltd. Reproduced by permission of the
          publishers
6.1(a)   Sebastian Forbes, *Sonata-Rondo* for Piano (1996), Theme a,
          start of first occurrence (section 1)   88
6.1(b)   Sebastian Forbes, *Sonata-Rondo* for Piano (1996), Theme a,
          final occurrence (section 24)   88

6.2(a) Sebastian Forbes, *Sonata-Rondo* for Piano (1996), Theme b,
first occurrence (section 2)   89
6.2(b) Sebastian Forbes, *Sonata-Rondo* for Piano (1996), Theme b,
final occurrence (section 25)   90
6.3(a) Sebastian Forbes, *Sonata-Rondo* for Piano (1996), Theme c,
start of first occurrence (section 4)   92
6.3(b) Sebastian Forbes, *Sonata-Rondo* for Piano (1996), Theme c,
start of later occurrence (section 22)   92
6.4(a) Sebastian Forbes, *Sonata-Rondo* for Piano (1996), Theme d,
first occurrence (section 5)   93
6.4(b) Sebastian Forbes, *Sonata-Rondo* for Piano (1996), Theme d,
later occurrence (section 17)   94
6.5(a) Sebastian Forbes, *Sonata-Rondo* for Piano (1996), Theme e,
start of first occurrence (section 9)   95
6.5(b) Sebastian Forbes, *Sonata-Rondo* for Piano (1996), Theme e,
start of later occurrence (section 21)   96
6.6   Sebastian Forbes, *Sonata-Rondo* for Piano (1996), Theme g,
third occurrence (section 16)   97
6.7   Sebastian Forbes, *Sonata-Rondo* for Piano (1996), Theme f,
first occurrence (section 7)   98
6.8   Sebastian Forbes, *Sonata-Rondo* for Piano (1996), Theme h,
third occurrence (section 18)   101
6.9   Alan Rawsthorne, First Piano Concerto, opening of second
movement   104
        © Oxford University Press 1945. Extract reproduced by
permission
6.10   Schubert, *Trout* Quintet, second movement, central cadence   105
6.11   Schubert, *Trout* Quintet, tonal plan of second movement   106
11.1   Alan Rawsthorne, *Madame Chrysenthème*, theme at start and
close of ballet.
        Extract reproduced by permission of Oxford University
Press   160

Notes on Contributors

Robert Adlington is Lecturer in Music at the University of Nottingham. He has written widely on twentieth-century music, with a particular focus on recent British music. He is the author of *The Music of Harrison Birtwistle* (CUP, 2000), and has published articles on Rebecca Saunders in *Musical Times* and the revised edition of the *New Grove*. Musical temporality forms a related interest: articles on this topic have appeared in *Music Analysis* and *Repercussions*. Recent writings include essays on 'Music Theatre since 1960', Birtwistle's *Gawain* and the Australian Fluxus revivalists 'SLAVE PIANOS'. A study of Louis Andriessen's *De Staat* will appear in Ashgate's series 'Landmarks in Music Since 1950'.

Sebastian Forbes studied at the Royal Academy of Music and then at Cambridge University, and is Professor and Director of Music at the University of Surrey. In addition to a wide range of teaching activities (including PhD by Composition), his varied musical activities have encompassed conducting and studio production. He is principally a composer, represented by over four decades of commissioned and prize-winning works. Among recent examples are Reflections (IAO Conference, Oxford, 1998), and String Quartet No. 5 and Sonata for 15 (15 solo strings), composed with the aid of research leave funded by the AHRB (Arts and Humanities Research Board). In progress is Duo for clarinet and piano.

Julian Johnson is an author and composer. He has written widely on historical and aesthetic issues in nineteenth- and twentieth-century music, particularly Mahler and the 2nd Viennese School and the work of T.W. Adorno. He is the author of two books: *Webern and the Transformation of Nature* (CUP, 1999) and *Who Needs Classical Music?* (OUP, 2002). His music has been performed throughout the UK and Europe and has been broadcast by the BBC. After teaching at the University of Sussex for nine years, he is now Fellow in Music at St Anne's College, Oxford.

Peter O'Hagan is Reader in Music at University of Surrey Roehampton, where he lectures on contemporary music. He is also a pianist, and has commissioned several works from British composers as well as giving numerous recitals of the contemporary repertoire in the UK, Europe and the USA. His principal area of academic research is the music of Pierre Boulez, and as well as publishing articles on Boulez's music, he has recently performed unpublished material from the Third Sonata with the composer's permission.

Ateş Orga, formerly Lecturer in Music at the University of Surrey, 1975–90, is Director of Music Administration Studies at the Dr Erol Üçer Center for Advanced Musical Research (MIAM), Istanbul Technical University. Active as a writer and recording producer specializing in pianists, conductors and contemporary music, he received a Royal Philharmonic Society Music Award for his 1993 Wigmore Hall series 'Piano Masterworks' created for Nikolai Demidenko and recorded on the Hyperion label.

Caroline Potter is Senior Lecturer in Music at Kingston University. A specialist in French music since Debussy, she is the author of *Henri Dutilleux* (Ashgate, 1997), and is currently editing a book on French music since Berlioz, also for Ashgate. Other current projects include a book on Nadia and Lili Boulanger.

Keith Potter is Senior Lecturer in Music at Goldsmiths College, University of London. He is the author of many articles on twentieth-century topics, particularly British and American music, and the author of *Four Musical Minimalists: La Monte Young, Terry Riley, Steve Reich, Philip Glass* (CUP, 2000). The founding editor of the contemporary music journal *Contact*, he is presently a regular contributor to *The Independent* newspaper. He was convenor and organizer of the Second Biennial International Conference on Twentieth-Century Music held at Goldsmiths College in 2001.

Edwin Roxburgh's music has been performed, broadcast and televised in many countries, most recently his Clarinet Concerto with Gervase de Peyer and the BBC Philharmonic Orchestra which the composer conducted. Commissions include the orchestral work *Montage* for the Proms in 1977, the oratorio *The Rock* for the Three Choirs Festival in 1980 and several films in the BBC's 'The World About Us' television series. In 1978 he was awarded a Collard Fellowship and in 1980 he was awarded the Cobbett Medal for services to chamber music. He is currently the Associate Composer of the London Festival Orchestra. The Royal Liverpool Philharmonic Orchestra, the City of Birmingham Symphony Orchestra and the Philharmonia are among the orchestras he has conducted. His music is published by UMP, Ricordi and Maecenas.

Arnold Whittall is Emeritus Professor of Music Theory and Analysis, King's College, London. His main publications are in the field of nineteenth-century German music, and also of twentieth-century composition and music theory. These include *Schoenberg's Chamber Music* (BBC, 1972), *Music since the First World War* (Dent, 1977/1988) revised and extended as *Musical Composition in the Twentieth Century* (OUP, 1999), *The Music of Britten and Tippett* (CUP, 1982/1990) and *The Music of Jonathan Harvey* (Faber and Faber, 1999). His many articles include major studies of Wagner, Strauss, Webern and Stravinsky, and his particular interest in contemporary music is reflected in substantial essays on Peter Maxwell Davies, Harrison Birtwistle and Nicholas Maw.

Acknowledgements

The publishers and the editor would like to thank the Governors of Southlands College, University of Surrey Roehampton, for their financial support of this book. We are grateful to the following publishers for their permission to feature music examples: Boosey & Hawkes Music Publishers Ltd and Universal Edition (London) Ltd (Harrison Birtwistle), Faber Music (Jonathan Harvey and Thomas Adès) and Edition Peters (James Dillon). We would also like to thank Sebastian Forbes and Edwin Roxburgh for their photographs, Maurice Foxall for permission to reproduce the photographs of Jonathan Harvey and Thomas Adès, Richard Kalina for permission to reproduce the photograph of Harrison Birtwistle, and Dylan Collard for permission to reproduce the photograph of James Dillon.

Introduction

Peter O'Hagan

This book is the product of a conference held early in 1999 at University of Surrey Roehampton. The intention was to bring together composers and academics in a forum in which issues of musical style and language could be addressed in context. The conference formed part of the final day of a series of concerts featuring British music of the last decade, in which several first performances took place, and it was rounded off by a concert given by the Arditti String Quartet devoted to music by four of the composers featured in this book – Thomas Adès, Harrison Birtwistle, James Dillon and Jonathan Harvey.

Perhaps it is a reflection of the bewildering stylistic plurality of the contemporary musical scene that the musicological certainties which categorized so much of the music of the preceding decades are increasingly challenged. Thus, Arnold Whittall's keynote address, in its subtly argued introduction to a consideration of recent music by James Dillon and Thomas Adès, called into question the pursuit of identifying stylistic influences as being, at least in part, a speculative activity. Implicit in the identification of 'influence' – and its obverse, 'originality' – is a unitary concept of musical history, which seems increasingly irrelevant to the more stylistically diverse decade on which the present volume is focused. If the decay of traditional tonality in the first decade of the century was accompanied by a shattering of the concept of stylistic progress, then it is also the case that the century's most radical figure, Schoenberg, was gradually absorbed into both romantic and neoclassical views of musical history – a process which Schoenberg did nothing to discourage in his own writings. It was the fate of his pupil, Webern, to be analysed and reinterpreted by the post-war generation in an audacious attempt both to legitimize their innovations while at the same time seeking to place their own music in a historical context. Such concerns seem strangely removed from those of many present day composers, as typified by Harrison Birtwistle's resistance to acknowledging even the background presence of Beethoven's *Grosse Fuge* in his own 'Todesfuge' during the course of an interview with Robert Adlington. Arnold Whittall's identification of allusion, as distinct from influence, as being of prime importance in much recent British music is demonstrated by the range of musical allusions he uncovers in Adès' *Arcadiana* and Dillon's Third String Quartet. The point is confirmed both by Dillon's acknowledgement in interview of the background presence of Scottish folk music and his reluctance to concede any direct

Bartókian references. As Whittall cautions in his conclusion: 'when musicologists – analysts – come to consider the particular composition, the allusions they uncover are as much to do with their own predispositions as with those of the composer'.

These observations are particularly pertinent given the richness and diversity of allusion which is characteristic of much British music from the 1960s onwards, and which to some extent replaces the imperative of an earlier generation to seek a specifically English historical context in which to work. Thus Maxwell Davies's appropriation of technical procedures derived from English medieval music appeared at the time to place him alongside such senior figures as Britten in his acknowledged indebtedness to Purcell's word-setting, and Tippett's absorption of the Elizabethan madrigal style. The violent expressionism of such works as *Eight Songs for a Mad King* appeared less disconcerting when placed in this context, despite the ironic allusions to such diverse sources as the foxtrot and the Victorian oratorio tradition. In Tippett's music of the 1970s, allusion plays an increasingly prominent role, *The Knot Garden*, for example, teeming with references to jazz on the one hand and to Beethoven and Schubert on the other. If Maxwell Davies's later music has shown a tendency to reclaim, on his own terms, the ground of the classical symphony and concerto, the 1970s is also a decade of more specific allusions to the German classical and romantic tradition, especially in the music of two of the most prominent emerging composers of those years, Robin Holloway and Nicholas Maw. The music of the succeeding generation of British composers has shown a continuing willingness to embrace a wide range of external sources. As Justin Connolly has pointed out,[1] the incorporation of elements of Schumann and Debussy in Oliver Knussen's *Ophelia Dances,* and Mark Anthony Turnage's allusions in *Before Dark* to Britten's *Turn of the Screw,* are paralleled by Simon Bainbridge's appropriation of minimalist techniques in *Concertante and Moto Perpetuo* and Jonathan Lloyd's uninhibited use of popular dance idioms in *Three Dances.*

That the stylistic diversity characteristic of the last two decades of the twentieth century is not without its dangers is suggested by the content of two of the papers during the first session of the Roehampton Conference. Julian Johnson began by observing the stylistic plurality of the contemporary musical scene, and developed his argument into a critique of the erosion of values implicit in much current thinking about music. This theme was developed by Edwin Roxburgh, and broadened into a discussion in which the state of music education and the vexed issue of funding of the Arts was discussed in the context of his own *Galileo* project. There has been no attempt to edit the polemical tone of these papers when preparing them for publication: the issues they confront are contentious ones and are inextricably linked with the stylistic tendencies of the decade.

The conference ended with a round-table discussion chaired by Arnold Whittall, to which Thomas Adès, Jonathan Harvey and James Dillon contributed. It was not possible to make a transcript of this discussion, and in the present volume it is replaced by a series of interviews with composers featured in the conference. In addition to these contributions, an interview was sought with Thomas Adès, but the extent of his other commitments made it impossible to arrange this by the time the volume was ready to go to press.

Although interviewers were encouraged to take an individual, rather than a prescriptive approach, similar concerns are revealed in this series of conversations. Thus, as James Dillon states with characteristic directness: 'I have no interest in being consistent, only radical ... there will always be a degree of self-organization in a musical form', a view echoed in Jonathan Harvey's remark: 'Having worked very hard to learn a craft I want this feeling now of breaking out, of just doing nothing according to any rules I know.' Edwin Roxburgh affirms the primacy of the imagination in the assertion: 'Composition is an adventure of discovery as much as invention', while at the same time qualifying his stance with the acknowledgement of the necessity that, 'the material itself is consistent within its structure'.

It is at first sight paradoxical that, at a time when many composers are uninhibitedly embracing a wide range of external sources, considerations of internal structure remain of prime concern to the five composers interviewed in this book. Thus in the course of a discussion of musical form in his *Sonata-Rondo,* Sebastian Forbes distinguishes the various techniques of internal allusion from pure repetition. The processes analysed by Forbes are closely paralleled in James Dillon's discussion of the transformation of two distinct pitch arrangements, a technique with a potential to act as a substitute for the key modulation of traditional tonality. Such transformation is a recurring theme in Jonathan Harvey's discussion of his recent music:

> the process of treating these isolated objects becomes a formal one because as the work progresses they're actually made to lose this Cagean object-nature and to split apart and decompose and begin to bleed into each other and become connected in long lines as if they're melted down and made into something, like metal made into a beautiful bowl.

In this context, Julian Johnson's penetrating study of Jonathan Harvey's recent music identifies another area of musical allusion – the relationship of a work to the rest of the composer's oeuvre. Not only are there the references to the sound world of Webern's Op. 9 and 10 – openly acknowledged by Harvey in interview as a major source of inspiration – but, on another level, the references to, and quotations from, his own music. No observer of the contemporary musical scene can fail to be struck by the extent to which self-allusion has become an increasingly important element in the music of composers to whom stylistic consistency is a major concern. Such internal allusions, characteristic of many major contemporary figures, are at first sight in opposition to the stylistic diversity of the music of the last decade. Yet, the two tendencies are to some extent complementary. One thinks of Maxwell Davies's fondness for a range of musical allusions, matched by his tendency to compose groups of thematically related works, while

Harrison Birtwistle's defining operatic masterpiece of the 1980s, *The Mask of Orpheus,* continues to resonate in other vocal and instrumental works of the same period. As Birtwistle put it in another context: 'I've always found writing music an evolutionary process ... that things tend to happen, and in one way, it's ... one piece that's evolving'.[2]

It will be evident from the above that this volume, in concentrating on the work of six composers during the last decade of the twentieth century, does not attempt anything more than a partial survey of British music during the period. The stylistic pluralities, identified by several speakers at the conference as an integral part of the contemporary musical scene, would demand a volume far beyond the scale and intentions of the present one. The presence of the Arditti Quartet, and its accomplishments in bringing into the public arena some of the most challenging and complex of contemporary scores, helped to provide parameters for the choice of music on which the conference focused. Having stated that, it is also evident from the series of interviews in this book that none of the composers can be labelled in a way which would admit ready categorization. Nevertheless, the issues raised here both with regard to the environment in which composers work and their relationship to the creative process itself are universal ones. If the volume assists in stimulating further discussion of these issues, it will have served its purpose.

Notes

1   Introduction to 'Music in our Time', BBC Radio 3, 5 April 1984.
2   Harrison Birtwistle in conversation with Anthony Burton, broadcast during the Interval of a concert from The Maltings. Snape as part of the 1991 Aldeburgh Festival, BBC Radio 3. 19 June 1991.

PART I
ESSAYS

Chapter 1

James Dillon, Thomas Adès, and the Pleasures of Allusion

Arnold Whittall

The 1990s are still too recent for all but the most self-assured critic or musicologist to offer a confident assessment of compositional profit and loss. Talk of a decade which sustained or even enhanced the typically late-modern pluralism of the twentieth century's last quarter may therefore be both premature and bland, but it is not necessarily misguided. For many close followers of the British scene, their most potent memories will be of a diversity vividly realized in the consolidation of three particular reputations: in order of age, Harrison Birtwistle, John Tavener and Mark-Anthony Turnage. The suggestion here of two wings and a centre can easily be fleshed out with other names – composers who can be made to fit into the avant-garde, minimalist and mainstream pigeonholes respectively. The outcome is a sense of a well-balanced variety, the extremes set off against the middle. But to deem this a healthy state of affairs is to risk accusations of complacency from those who think differently.

Musicologists with aspirations to double as cultural historians have long since latched on to the notion of the steady state, a circumstance in which late-modern pluralism waxes and wanes as various fashions come and go. The obvious dangers of steady states are predictability and monotony: and with late-modernism well established from at least the 1970s, it is not difficult to contrast what some will characterize as the wearily unnaughty 1990s with those deliciously naughty 1890s. Any attempt to argue that the 1990s was actually a rather satisfying and even an exciting decade can easily meet with derision from those with other axes to grind. But the supporters of a status quo expect to be derided as complacent or even corrupt by those who are passionately committed to an alternative attitude; and if you genuinely believe that the past is another country, the present boring and the future bleak, no composer and no commentator can prove you right or wrong. What composers and commentators can do is to use their narrower perspectives to explore different, less grandly synoptic or ideologically fraught agendas; and my agenda here is to explore two satisfying, even exciting British works for string quartet from the 1990s – the third quartet (1998) by James Dillon (b. 1950), and *Arcadiana* (1994) by Thomas Adès (b. 1971) – by means of a blend of formalist and hermeneutic interpretative strategies. These particular works may fret against the artificial boundaries of the well-balanced three-part

1   Thomas Adès

model outlined in my first paragraph, but this need not require outright rejection of that schema. If it becomes a notional background rather than an all-determining foreground, its value might even be enhanced.

One important musicologist with her finger on the pulse of contemporary cultural practice, Rose Rosengard Subotnik, has commented on the recent tendency of musicology to move away from what she calls 'technical descriptions and analyses toward images and analogies and ideas', as part of 'a massive process of western self-criticism' whose 'immediate target was not music; it was reason'.[1] But many of us are perfectly happy to move self-critically towards 'images, analogies and ideas' as long as we can bring an element of technical description and analysis with us. It is not so much a matter of moving away from something as of placing that 'something' in a wider context, and this is one reason why the second part of my title is not, for example, 'and the resonance of tonal models'.

Readers 'in the know' will suspect that reference to 'the pleasures of allusion' involves an element of ideological confrontation with 'the anxiety of influence'. One of my objects is certainly to take issue with attempts, like those of the American musicologist Joseph Straus, to contextualize music analysis by reference to Harold Bloom's neo-Freudian ideas about indebtedness, guilt and fear – or at least with attempts to replace all other interpretative strategies with just this, Bloomian, one:[2] and I am aligning myself with the most rigorous and persuasive critique of that strategy yet published, by Richard Taruskin.[3]

Straus, following Bloom, defines 'the anxiety of influence' as 'the ambivalence a poet may feel toward an overwhelming and potentially stultifying tradition' – 'a fear of being swallowed up or annihilated by one's towering predecessors'.[4] Put like this, the tone is indeed that of bargain-basement Freud, and Straus moves all too easily from the general to the particular, in which various kinds of references and allusions – for example, to Bach by Berg in his Violin Concerto – are characterized as 'misreadings'. Taruskin's view is not that Bloom's theories and analytical techniques are a bad thing – rather that they are misrepresented, misread, in Straus's work. Taruskin believes that the kind of overt modelling examined by Straus in the Berg example is a displacement of the true 'anxiety of influence', and he feels that Straus is a more convincing Bloomian when, for example, he considers Stravinsky's veiled appropriation of aspects of Chopin's second Ballade in the first movement of the *Serenade in A*.

My problem with this is my problem with all ideas about influences as things which can be definitively identified, the layers of deceptive originality stripped away to reveal the naked, shivering model beneath. If, as Taruskin declares, 'a strong misreader irrepressibly represses the old to produce the new',[5] that process of repression involves the composer in such an intimate and intricate relationship with the past that direct representations of materials from the past will be notable for their absence, and ultimately inaccessible to analysis. Of course, we can indulge in as much informed speculation about sources and influences as we like, and it seems to me that far too much valuable musicological time is devoted to doing just that.

Taruskin also objects that Straus's misreading of Bloom leads him to propose an essentially 'decorous model' of influence, 'centering not on uncontrollable belligerent contest' as Bloom argues, 'but on voluntary, benign submission, described by T.S. Eliot as the poet's "surrender of himself ... to something which is more valuable"'.[6] It might appear that what I am calling the pleasure of allusion is precisely this more decorous model of influence. But that is not quite the case. My own view is that, when Thomas Adès alludes to Mozart, Schubert and, possibly, Elgar in the movement titles of his *Arcadiana*, he is not 'doing an Eliot' and surrendering himself to something he sees as more valuable, more venerable, than his own creativity. In my judgement (Adès might tell us differently, of course) he makes these references, these allusions, without any hang-ups, because he finds it pleasurable to do so; and (I presume) he hopes that listeners will share that pleasure. Anxiety, fear, guilt or even reverence, have nothing to do with it; nor do I believe that Adès is allowing certain associations to be evident the more deviously to suppress the ones which really matter. Similarly, the possible – and possibly ironic – allusions in Dillon's third quartet to the multi-movement 'symphonic' tradition of the genre which culminated in Bartók can be deemed both playful and aggressive, but guilt or fear in face of such hallowed but redundant traditions play no part in Dillon's virtuosic 'misreading'.

Bloomians cannot escape the simplistic binary oppositions that stem from their hero's thinking. What, for example, are we to make of the assertion that 'to read is to be dominated; to misread is to assert one's own priority'?[7] It seems to me that composers are far more likely to be motivated by a mixture of contrasting and competing impulses, and while anxiety may certainly be a part of the creative process – concern about what certain things will actually sound like, whether they will work, whether the audience will get the point – the predominant reason for composing is that it satisfies the desire for communication through self-expression. Without wishing to yield totally to the aura of Roland Barthes and those who concern themselves with 'the pleasure of the text',[8] it must surely be conceded that creating a text satisfies desire and causes pleasure – to the creator, if to no one else? I should add at this point that I myself take pleasure in not using the term 'allusion' in its narrowest, most precise sense as 'passing or indirect reference'. As I use it here, 'allusion' stands for a rich range of procedures from passing, elusive hints, to explicit, extended references and even quotations. What links these procedures is the multivalence of their reception, the probability that they will mean different things to everyone who is aware of them.

Neither James Dillon nor Thomas Adès can exactly be accused of favouring essentially English rather than more cosmopolitan musical aesthetics. But this does not mean that concepts involving nationality are irrelevant to their work. Dillon was born and educated (partly) in Scotland, and earlier commentators duly accorded him 'outsider' status, noting the element of 'sheer aggression' as well as 'a sense of struggle, of wrestling with intractable material' which suggests Varèse and even Beethoven as 'obvious' ancestors.[9] In his characteristically penetrating discussion Richard Toop does not pursue the modernist/classical dialectic implied by this comparison, but hints instead at a distinction between Northern intransigence and the 'unusually Mediterranean opulence' of *helle Nacht* (1986–87).[10] This is especially resonant, given the way in which Toop's dialogue with Dillon moves on to identify the absence of 'mediation' – the 'abruption' – they admire in Xenakis.[11] Eventually, this idea transmutes into 'this kind of moment when things are between order and disorder', another elementally modernist perception, ultimately deriving from 'this whole problem, that we grapple with in music, between difference and invariance'.[12] The tension between tendencies not only to promote synthesis but also to reject it might therefore be one of the defining factors of the way in which *Überschreiten* (1986) reflects its Rilke-inspired preoccupation with 'fusion of the organic and the transcendental' alongside that 'dissident ... excess, rebellion and transgression in the face of order' which are no less salient.[13]

Such matters are the common currency of critical attempts to place a composer who struggles with 'this notion of cohesion',[14] and who acknowledges essential aspects of tradition only to challenge them: thus, in the first quartet (1983) 'I wanted to create a kind of notion of directionality in terms of discontinuities ... I was maintaining the notion of a traditional narrative, but ... through disruption rather than through continuity'.[15] Another version of the same concept appears in Dillon's unpublished notes on *Introitus* (1989–90), one of the *Nine rivers* pieces, which draws attention to the opposition between 'river' as something that flows and 'river' as someone who disrupts. That the alternative dialectic involving the modernist/classical (Varèse/Beethoven) opposition might nevertheless remain relevant is suggested by Dillon's preference for textures dominated by homogeneities which 'may be resisted, but ... are ultimately reinforced'.[16] However, such reinforcement has little or nothing to do with classical notions of resolution, just as Dillon's acknowledgement of nationality has little or nothing to do with quoting folk or folk-like material. It all comes down to persistent instability. As Dillon has said, 'if you live on the west coast of Scotland, it is impossible to have a rosy view of nature: it's forever in flux'.[17] Dillon's music shuns the kind of unmediated references to Scottish musical topics found in such Scottish or Scotland-based composers as James MacMillan and Peter Maxwell Davies. What can be found – in the case of the third string quartet, in particular – is music whose arsenal of allusion is less explicit, but, I would argue, no less fundamental, and can be traced at core to a kind of confrontation between cultivated and popular traditions that is intensely unstable in structure and unremittingly dark in tone.

While preparing this chapter I came across a recently published essay by Daniel Chua called 'Haydn as Romantic: a chemical experiment with instrumental music'. Writing about Haydn's Quartet in C, Op. 54, No. 2, Chua unveils 'a catalogue of quirks, with its mischievous gaps, harmonic fissures, asymmetrical structures and stark juxtapositions', and he comments more generally on how 'Haydn's evocations of bucolic drones and folk tunes are quirky, decontextualised objects that dispossess nature of its innocence ... Semiotics for Haydn is not a means of making meaning but of destabilizing representation'.[18] Given that Chua's agenda here involves an attempt to bring Haydn within an aesthetic and technical framework appropriate to modernism, rather than what is conventionally understood as classicism, it does not seem to me too absurd to note the relevance of his comments to Dillon. Not only the harmonic fissures and stark juxtapositions, but the evocation of bucolic drones as quirky, decontextualized objects that deprive nature of its innocence – all these correspond very directly to things which I hear in Dillon's third quartet. More specifically, the music

Example 1.1   James Dillon, Third String Quartet, 3rd movement from bar 30

seems to generate an extended dance of rough vitality and rage – Toop's 'sheer aggression' again – by way of confrontation between an allusion to the culti-vated tradition, as in the passages of four-part counterpoint most evident in the third movement (Example 1.1), and, as in the end of the same movement,

Example 1.1 continued

allusion to something, basically homophonic, which goes beyond or behind cultivation (the implied double canon) to rediscover that cleansing yet disorientating primitivism so vital to the early phase of twentieth-century modernism (Example 1.2). Drones, blunt repetitions, glissandos, microtonal inflections, and

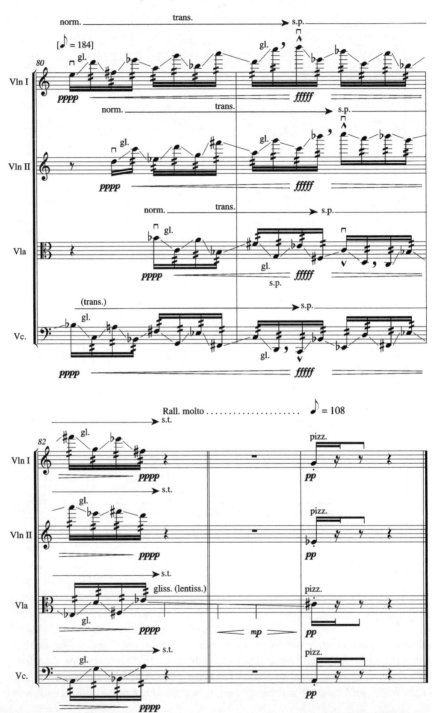

Example 1.2   James Dillon, Third String Quartet, 3rd movement, ending

a style of playing that shuns the vibrato-based sweetness of the quartet tradition: these are the predominant features of the Dillon style in this piece, and they come across as particularly vital offshoots of that 'weird, phantasmagoric' atmosphere 'with moments of downright ugliness not excluded'[19] so palpable in the Rimbaud-inspired materials of *Nine rivers*'s 'L'oeuvre au noir' (1990).

Dillon is a composer who, whether by accident or design, is able to satisfy the need for allusion while not diluting his commitment to an idiom that distances itself from tradition. In my brief, 1993 discussion of his then ongoing *Nine rivers* series, I argued that 'with his reliance on morphological, anatomical and hydro-logical metaphors, Dillon seems especially excited by the possibility of animating the flow of textures by degrees of smoothness and turbulence' – rather, that is, than by abrupt juxtapositions and disorientating discontinuities. In the same context I quoted Phil Lesh's comment that, in Dillon, 'there seem to be no easily discernible strata or layers, as in the music of Carter or Birtwistle, but rather a continuously transforming polychromatic curtain of sound'.[20] Now it would be remarkable indeed if a composer were to take such comments so seri-ously as to set out, deliberately, to contradict them. So I am not suggesting that Dillon is, as it were, alluding to Lesh in the third quartet, despite the fact that discernible strata or layers are essential and powerful features of the music's sustained dialogue between medium and message, in another, even more deter-mined demonstration of his concern with 'a kind of ... directionality in terms of discontinuities'.[21] This work – the music at once raw and cooked – offers a particularly cogent discourse on the topics of stratification versus co-ordination, divergence versus convergence, and also, last but not least, between floating and focused treatments of harmonic texture. The opening of the first movement announces some of these themes (Example 1.3). The surging, vibratoless sound is raw and immediate, and the initial proposition is not simply a matter of two pairs of instruments setting different agendas, one about constrained yet evolving melody, the other about rooted harmony. The simple exclusiveness with which one pair encloses the other is too primitive a notion not to invite early destabiliza-tion; and the movement's second textural state involves trills, tremolos and a sense of common purpose, not least with respect to the suggestion that middle D has focal status (Example 1.4).

The focal status of middle D is also a central topic of the second movement (Example 1.5 juxtaposes the beginning and the ending). Here the use of homo-phonic reiteration as a force to constrain and even suppress attempts at melodic, decorative dispersal, dredges up the possibility of allusion to the past master of such strategies in the quartet medium, Bartók. This is the moment to ask the leading question lying behind my entire argument. Who is doing the alluding, and finding pleasure in doing so? Is it the composer, or is it the analyst? To single out Dillon's Ds for special emphasis is to respond to a 'fact' about his music, but what does it mean to argue that, because Bartók also stressed Ds in a rhythmically brittle way – see, especially, the middle movement of his second quartet – Dillon

Example 1.3   James Dillon, Third String Quartet, 1st movement, opening

is referring to Bartók? Sensing some similarity in this matter is very much the small change of critical reception; yet because it serves more to distance Dillon from Bartók than to demonstrate an abject, fearful dependency, it can open up a whole treasure chest of analytical enterprises. It also shows that the possibility of

* Violins should emerge as overtones from the v'cello pedal-tone.

** move continuously between a s.p. position and on the bridge to create
varying degrees of noise.
All movement should be irregular and not in unison with the dynamics.

Example 1.4   James Dillon, Third String Quartet, 1st movement from bar 54

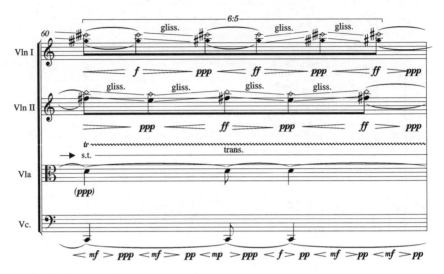

Example 1.4   continued

allusion to a certain number of structural and stylistic associations is one way in
which the composer can contribute something personal to the string quartet genre,
and that without needing to be completely and irrevocably separated off from the
quartet tradition.

   There is an interesting comparison to be made between the savage dance of
Dillon's third quartet and that which forms the central movement of *Arcadiana* by
Thomas Adès, and whose title, the single word 'Et' (from 'Et in arcadia ego'), is
followed in brackets by the generic marker 'tango mortale'. The melodic,
rhythmic and harmonic materials of the Adès piece (Example 1.6 shows its beginning) are all much more explicitly redolent of earlier laments, dances of death,
and of a bitterness as ironic as it is suicidal, than is the case with Dillon; and the
broader context within which the Adès movement is found also serves to under-
line the tango's generic status as a character piece whose guise of savagery is just
one possible costume among many.

   Focusing on the Dillon of the third quartet, rather than of *La femme invisible*
(1989) or *Vernal Showers* (1992), downplays those aspects of textural warmth
and even delicacy which bring him just a little closer to more 'mainstream'
musical qualities. Even at his most lyrical, however, Dillon cannot be brought
alongside Adès, just as Adès at his most complex cannot be brought alongside
Dillon. Their worlds are more complementary than contiguous, though it might
be hazarded that Dillon's quizzical angle on national (Scottish) primitivism is
paralleled by Adès's no less quizzical angle on English reticence. Adès, a
phenomenon of the 1990s on the British musical scene, is at his most arresting
when he casts a central European (if not explicitly Hungarian) shadow over the
North London-cum-Cambridge sophistications with which his music often seems

II

Example 1.5(a)   James Dillon, Third String Quartet, 2nd movement, opening

most immediately at home. As with Dillon, therefore, disorientation and instability are of the essence. But Adès is the more 'mainstream' in that compositions tend to embody that characteristic twentieth-century obsession with the past as another country within which we can discern the elements of new worlds. For example, his piano piece of 1992, *Darknesse visible*, is described by Adès as 'an explosion of Dowland's lute song "In darknesse let me dwell"; no notes have been added' to the Dowland: 'indeed, some have been removed. Patterns latent in the original have been isolated and regrouped, with the aim of illuminating the song from within, as if during the course of a performance'.[22] Similar processes, of isolating and regrouping elements from specific models, can be found in

Example 1.5(b)   **James Dillon, Third String Quartet, 2nd movement, ending**

Arcadiana, and the sixth movement, 'O Albion' (Example 1.7), has particular resonance in the light of my concerns in this chapter.

As Adès has said, 'each of the seven titles which comprise *Arcadiana* evokes an image associated with ideas of the idyll, vanishing, vanished or imaginary' and he describes 'O Albion' as one of two movements which 'inhabit pastoral Arcadias'.[23] It is easy to concur with Andrew Porter that, in 'O Albion', 'seventeen *devotissimo* bars in E flat major, the key of "Nimrod", pay tender, nostalgic

Example 1.6   Thomas Adès, *Arcadiana*, 4th movement, opening

Example 1.7   Thomas Adès, *Arcadiana*, 6th movement, opening

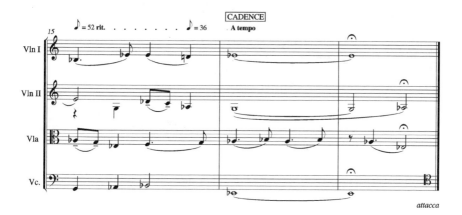

Example 1.7 continued

homage to Elgar and his England'.[24] Apart from the apparent tonality, Adès begins with a G natural (2nd violin), held over from the previous movement: his bass line then moves from E flat to C and on to G, just like Elgar's. More broadly, Adès's division of his motivic material between rising and falling shapes, and his use of sequence, are explicitly Elgarian features. We can clarify the motivic content of 'O Albion', and its Elgarian profile, by detaching those rising and falling shapes from the harmonic and contrapuntal context Adès provides (Example 1.8). If we label the ascending material 'A' and the descending 'D', as shown in Example 1.8, we can summarize the form of 'O Albion' as A, D, A1, A2, D1, D2 and cadence (see, again, Example 1.7). More than that, we can construct a hypothetical Elgarian model for 'O Albion' by filling out this A and D material in orthodox tonal style (Example 1.9). The result is the kind of music

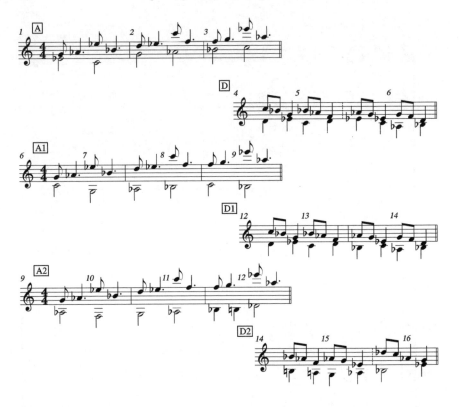

Example 1.8   Thomas Adès, *Arcadiana*, 6th movement (motivic elements)

that could just have found its place as the noble second theme of a 'Pomp and Circumstance' march.

But the main purpose of this analytical exercise is to reinforce the point that 'O Albion' itself is not and could not be by Elgar; its entire linguistic and generic character marks a relation to a model as much (if not more) in terms of forgetting, or distancing, as of remembering. This is clear from the simple initial difference – the G Adès holds over from the previous movement is an octave below Elgar's in 'Nimrod'; and the distancing in 'O Albion' gains strength until its final cadence, stratified between the straight E flat perfect cadence in the outer voices and the preference for A flat in the inner voices.

Throughout the piece the counterpoint creates levels of dissonance which inhibit the flow of Elgarian voice-leading: see, for example, how the clash of A flat against G in bar 1 carries over into the E flat/D natural clash of bar 2 (see Example 1.7 again). The result in 'O Albion' is an unstable diatonicism which consistently blocks the possibility of 'structural' or 'musicological' hearing, according to the precepts of functional harmony, however vivid its evocation of

Example 1.9 Thomas Adès, *Arcadiana*, 6th movement (hypothetical Elgarian model)

the 'sweetness of tonality'.[25] In consequence, I would suggest, listening to 'O Albion' addresses itself to ways of characterizing its materials which are less to do with traditional harmonic models than with generic prototypes. It could well be that the composer's own memory shifted at quite an early stage from the specifics of 'Nimrod' to the more general associative categories present in *Arcadiana* as a whole.

Like Schumann's *Kreisleriana*, subtitled 'eight fantasies', *Arcadiana* offers a collection of movements connected by reference to the topic or person identified. It is, nevertheless, not simply a sequence of seven idylls, in the normal sense of 'scenes of happy innocence or rustic simplicity', but involves the shadowing of its sources from a distance at which the musical identity of those sources may no longer be clear, and their generic associations may be questioned rather than confirmed. There is, therefore, little enlightenment to be gained from placing *Arcadiana* in the direct line of other musical idylls – those, for example, by Wagner, Janáček and Frank Bridge. Despite the association with pastoral, acknowledged by Adès, the individual titles for the seven pieces, and the musical materials and structures they employ, create a more intricate generic frame of reference than that embraced only by associations with the nexus around idyll and pastoral. In particular, I believe that it makes sense to view *Arcadiana* from a similar perspective to other contributions to the genre of what I will call the 'lyric suite', which includes not only Berg's six-movement composition for string quartet, but also Liszt's *Années de pèlerinage* collections and, more saliently for Adès, Britten's third quartet as well as his orchestral suite on English folk tunes, *A Time There Was*.

Berg's use of 'lyric' in his title is an explicit allusion to Zemlinsky's *Lyric Symphony*, and implies an emphasis on song-like melody and song-like forms, as well as acknowledging the suppressed text of the last movement. Similar concerns can be found in *Arcadiana*, which refers obliquely to vocal music by Mozart and Schubert, as well as to other musical evocations of night, water and death. There are also certain technical links between Berg and Adès. For example, the early stages of *Arcadiana*'s first and last movements ('Venezia notturna' and 'Lethe') organize their post-tonal harmony around perfect fifths (Example 1.10), and include lament-like phrases alongside dance-like song material. Berg's *Lyric Suite* charts an unambiguous progression from the genuine but unstable content-ment of its opening to the stark despair of the ending, But what seems to be the most essential quality of the idyll, in Adès's interpretation, is its unreality, the sense in which, the more we aspire to recapture untroubled contentment, the more difficult that process becomes. It is this quality, and the fundamental association between utopian aspirations and an inescapable if understated melancholia, as idyll and lament overlap and interact, which seem to me to determine the special character of 'O Albion' itself.

When it comes to interactions between idyll and lament, 'O Albion' might even be felt to acknowledge hymnic perspectives reaching back through 'Nimrod' and the Prelude to Act 3 of *Die Meistersinger*, to Beethoven's 'Cavatina' from the Quartet Op. 130. But such a generic background reinforces the technical point that Adès could not compose a full-blooded, Nimrod-like tonal climax without exploding his own stylistic ecosystem from within. Nor could he allude to the more austere atmosphere and refracted harmonies of a Stravinskian chorale, like that which ends *Symphonies of Wind Instruments*, without negating – betraying – the intensely romantic spirit that informs 'O Albion'. Whether or not the title makes an allusion to Blake's poetic epic 'Jerusalem, the Emanation of the Giant Albion', the music involves those 'more local fields' of 'a pastoral Arcadia' to which Adès refers in his notes, and we can, if we wish, think of the result as

(a) I. Venezia notturna

Example 1.10(a) Thomas Adès, *Arcadiana*, 1st movement, bars 1–3 and 9–11

(b) VII. Lethe

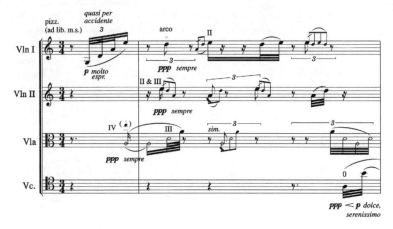

Example 1.10(b) Thomas Adès, *Arcadiana*, 7th movement, bars 1–3

involving a conjunction between what counts, in a very broad sense, as Stravinskian harmonic thinking, and a world of expression closer to Berg or even Britten – for example, the 'Solo' movement of the Third String Quartet.

When I was beginning to plan this chapter I came across Roger Marsh's article on Vic Hoyland in *Tempo* magazine for December 1998. Marsh declares: 'from the very beginning Hoyland's work has been astonishing in its originality'. This does not mean that no influences can be discerned, but rather that influences are both obvious and irrelevant. As Marsh says,

> Hoyland's appetite for influence, in fact, may be the key to his work – for his increasingly individual musical voice has never ceased to absorb new experience, to embrace and assimilate the world as he finds it and as it excites him. His great power, though, is precisely his ability to assimilate and process material, so that one is unlikely to mistake his purpose for some kind of post-modern collage.[26]

Something similar can be said of both Dillon and Adès, despite the very different connotations of tradition which apply to their works for string quartet. With Dillon there is pleasure to be gained from acknowledging his forceful confrontation of a genre – the 'classic' four-movement quartet – whose history we have no good reason to forget but whose procedures we have no good reason to reproduce. (Why are Dillon's movements in this order? Do they need to be?) With Adès's unsymphonic lyric suite, the play with genre may be less confrontational and therefore even more pleasurable – always assuming that it is more enjoyable not to be challenged as intensely as we are sure to be by Dillon's radicalism.

Where I part company with Roger Marsh is in his suggestion that establishing a composer's originality involves minimizing the significance of what he calls influences. At the end of the article Marsh quotes Hoyland himself, in an interview about his *Bagatelles for string quartet* of 1995, describing the piece in terms of 'shaking hands with other sorts of music'.[27] All I have been claiming here is that composers cannot really function without shaking hands – with other composers if not with musicologists. Their motives for doing so will invariably be mixed, and it may often be difficult, in these dark days of late-modernism, for them to be absolutely sure whether the person they are shaking hands with is who they really think it is. So, when musicologists – analysts – come to consider the particular composition, the allusions they uncover are as much to do with their own predispositions as with those of the composer. What is to be hoped is that, despite this division of identity, and of responsibility, composer and analyst can actually share in the communication of something significant. In the new millennium it seems likely that the critical interpretation of musical compositions will need ever more sensitive ways of exploring interactions between formal and hermeneutic strategies. To strive to exclude anxiety and fear from this process, and base it firmly and cheerfully on pleasure, enjoyment and enthusiasm, is a project worthy of a new era in which new music will probably remain no less beholden to old, or at least other, music than it has done up to now.

Notes

1 Rose Rosengard Subotnik, *Deconstructive Variations. Music and Reason in Western Society* (Minneapolis and London: University of Minnesota Press, 1996), p. xxv.
2 Joseph N. Straus, *Remaking the Past: Musical Modernism and the Influence of the Tonal Tradition* (Cambridge, Mass.: Harvard University Press, 1990); also 'The "Anxiety of Influence" in twentieth-century music', *Journal of Musicology*, vol. 9, no. 4 (Fall 1991), pp. 430–47. The principal texts by Harold Bloom are *The Anxiety of Influence: A Theory of Poetry* (New York: Oxford University Press, 1973), *A Map of Misreading* (Oxford: Oxford University Press, 1975), *Kaballah and Criticism* (New York: Seabury Press, 1975), and *Poetry and Repression: Revisionism from Blake to Stevens* (New Haven: CT. Yale University Press, 1976).
3 Richard Taruskin, 'Revising revision', *Journal of the American Musicological Society*, vol. 46, no. 1 (1993), pp. 114–138.
4 Straus, 'The Anxiety of Influence', p. 436.
5 Taruskin, 'Revising revision', p. 126.
6 Ibid., p. 116.
7 Straus, 'The Anxiety of Influence', p. 438.
8 Roland Barthes, *Image–Music–Text*, tr. Stephen Heath (London: Fontana, 1977), pp. 163–4.
9 Richard Toop, 'Four facets of the new complexity', *Contact*, no. 32 (Spring 1988), p. 38.
10 Ibid.
11 Ibid, p. 39.
12 Ibid, p. 41.
13 Ibid, p. 48.
14 See Keith Potter, 'James Dillon: currents of development', *Musical Times*, vol. 131, no. 1767 (May 1990), p. 253.
15 Ibid, p. 256.
16 Arnold Whittall, 'Riverrun: the music of James Dillon', *Musical Times*, vol. 134, no. 1805 (July 1993), p. 385.
17 See Richard Toop, 'Bright lights and alchemical fire', booklet with Auvidis Montaigne CD MO782038 (1995), p. 10.
18 Daniel K.L. Chua, 'Haydn as Romantic: a chemical experiment with instrumental music', in *Haydn Studies*, ed. W. Dean Sutcliffe (Cambridge: Cambridge University Press, 1998), pp. 149, 147.
19 Whittall, 'Riverrun', p. 387.
20 Ibid, p. 385. Phil Lesh's comments are in *Tempo*, vol. 182 (September 1992), pp. 42–3.
21 Potter, 'James Dillon', p. 256.
22 Thomas Adès, note in score of *Darknesse Visible* (London: Faber Music, 1998).

23 Thomas Adès, note in score of *Arcadiana* (London: Faber Music, 1995).

24 Andrew Porter, booklet with EMI Classics CD 5 72271 2 4 (1998), p. 4.

25 This phrase is used by Michael Cherlin in his article 'Memory and rhetorical trope in Schoenberg's string trio', *Journal of the American Musicological Society*, vol. 51, no. 3 (1998), p. 559.

26 Roger Marsh, 'Foxes and Vixens: an update on the music of Vic Hoyland', *Tempo*, vol. 207 (December 1998), p. 22.

27 Ibid, p. 27.

Chapter 2

Multiple Choice? Composing and Climate Change in the 1990s

Julian Johnson

There is a view that music changes only as a result of its own internal dynamic and is unaffected by what goes on around it in 'the real world'. Of course, this is no more true than the idea that plants or trees are unaffected by their environment. Organic forms grow according to predetermined codes but only inasmuch as external conditions remain relatively constant. When a weather system changes, certain plants no longer flourish while others come into their own. Some produce strange hybrid forms to adapt to the new conditions. Perhaps music works in similar ways: a musical style may seem to have a certain internal logic, yet is never entirely independent of the context in which it takes place. Towards the end of the twentieth century there were some clear signs of climate change in British music and it is perhaps to these that one should look for an explanation of changes in the music itself.

That the musical climate has been changing recently is common knowledge, of course: even those who venture out seldom will not have missed a wide range of climate change indicators. Consider, for example, the displacement of older systems caused by the launch in 1992 of Classic FM, a radio station predicated on the idea that classical music could fulfil some of the same functions as pop music if marketed in the right way. Its phenomenal success was guaranteed by the downplaying of certain long-standing claims about classical music – principally, the related ideas that classical music requires a degree of literacy and needs to be approached with an attitude of thoughtful concentration. BBC Radio 3, in order to survive the altered conditions, has shown obvious adaptations of its own, trying recently to throw its net wider and to offer programmes which deliberately cross traditional stylistic boundaries. So in compilation programmes now you are increasingly likely to hear 'daring' juxtapositions of Vaughan Williams and John Williams, Bach and Bacharach.

Similar new growths and changing forms are obvious in the world of musical performance. Performers themselves have changed; how well they do in the new climate seems to depend more than ever on the horticultural expertise of photographers, marketing and advertising people. What chance female singers or violinists who do not look good half-out of a ball gown, or male pianists who do not look a little damaged and interesting? Programmes themselves have been changing, especially in the delicate field of new music which is more susceptible than most to climate change. In order to survive, programmes have become more diverse and eclectic. As they have done so, old canons have begun to shrivel. In this context it is no longer a surprise to see, for example, that the directors of the South Bank's Meltdown Festival have included Elvis Costello, Laurie Anderson and John Harle as well as George Benjamin and Magnus Lindberg.

A highly specialized indicator of the effect of climate change on new British music is the Society for the Promotion of New Music (SPNM). The SPNM has been fairly central to British new music since its founding in 1943; indeed, that very centrality has been the cause of criticism from those who feel excluded from it. To get a sense of how climate change has altered the musical landscape one could do worse than look at how the activities of the SPNM differ now from 10 or 20 years ago. Consider SPNM's listings magazine, *new notes*. A few years ago it began using the front cover for a short article on some aspect of current music. These are deliberately not scholarly pieces but more direct statements from composers, performers and others involved in the production of new music. Perhaps one should not attach too much importance to these but they do, never-theless, reflect fairly directly many of the changing emphases and positions within British new music.

The front page of the issue that appeared in January 1999 was given over to an article called 'Now that's what I call "contemporary"' written by Beverley Crew, administrator of the Contemporary Music Network. Here she considers 'how radically perceptions of new and contemporary music have been changing over the past few years' and goes on to compare the anorak world of the new music concert a few years ago with the bright new world of contemporary music now. What defines the contemporary scene now, she suggests, is a wide and diverse range of musical styles – she lists, jazz, classical, world, electronic and experi-mental, as well as the more adventurous end of pop, rock and dance music. It is also distinguished, she adds, by more professional marketing, a better audience mix (in terms of gender) and a loosening up of the formal concert ritual.

Above all, the watchword here is diversity: more diverse music draws a more diverse audience. As an example she cites the diversity of music the Contempo-rary Music Network has promoted over the last 28 years, including the Steve Reich Ensemble, Gil Evans orchestra, Philip Glass Ensemble, Jan Garbarek Quartet and the Kronos Quartet. The programme for next season, she writes, 'is one of the most eclectic ever, including Jazz, Tango, Classical, Brazilian New Beat, Zappa, South African and Cameroonian World/Jazz, Asian Club, Multi-media Soundcircus, Folk and Japanese Sound and Image manipulation projects. Now that's what I call "contemporary"!'[1] The article is rounded off with a photo of the author which would not look out of place in *Vogue* magazine. The new music anorak is here replaced by a fur coat. The new contemporary scene is obvi-ously as stylish, sexy and exciting as the old one was awkward, academic and dull.[2]

In the following month's issue (February 1999) we hear about the latest version of the contemporary not from an administrator but, this time from composer, arranger and performer, Joby Talbot, who works simultaneously in several different fields – writing for television, 'classical' ensembles and writing, arranging and performing with the pop group Divine Comedy. His message endorses that of Beverley Crew: he is critical of the narrow-mindedness of some of the classical music fraternity and ends with a warning: 'People are often disparaging about the current musical climate but I can honestly say that I'd rather be working as a creative musician now than at any other time in history. I think all you people out there who still compartmentalise your music are seriously missing out.'[3]

Both these commentators conspicuously avoid addressing the difference between the idea of *new music* and that of *contemporary music*. This is significant because while *new* implies a selective judgement, *contemporary* – in a literal sense – is simply a comprehensive term for everything that is current. One is the result of aesthetic and musical distinctions, the other implies something more like a catalogue. In Beverley Crew's list, for example, the different musical types are not necessarily related by some common musical connection or quality; they are, rather, defined sociologically as interesting and worthy of note – a kind of magazine breakdown of what's in and what's out, a self-fulfilling listings guide to contemporary fashion.

The eclecticism promoted by this approach is not just to do with the *availability* of diverse musical practices; increasingly, it involves the eroding of barriers between them. In *new notes* of December 1998 Joanna MacGregor responded to November's front-page article – a discussion of the merits of acoustic versus electronic music. Her response expressed exasperation that, in 1998, we should be having such a polarized debate at all and in the course of her own discussion cited a range of work she admired from musicians as diverse as Talvin Singh, Bjork, Stockhausen, Jonathan Harvey, The Beatles and Massive Attack.[4]

Joanna MacGregor and Beverley Crew argue for a pluralism in which everyone is a winner, for a musical menu in which all tastes are catered for and that represents the work of all the chefs in the kitchen, a menu from which you can select any combination that takes your fancy. But the ideal of total inclusiveness proves difficult to realize. For many, the climate change is experienced as a thaw after a particularly harsh and long winter (one that began soon after the Second World War) or, to mix my metaphors, as comparable to the fall of a rather brutal and long-standing dictatorship. The celebration of new freedoms is mixed with recrimination and resentment as, after years of repression, people line up to denounce the old guard. Composers who felt ostracized by the style edicts of high modernism have suddenly found themselves in a period of musical *glasnost*; old idols are set to topple and some people it seems would gladly decapitate statues of Birtwistle or Boulez (had any been built). In some circles there is a collective purging going on, a self-flagellation for having been taken in by modernism that extends not only to composers but also to performers, academics and a host of cultural critics and journalists.

Also in *new notes* of December 1998 is a reproduced extract from a lecture given by Nicholas Kenyon at the Royal College of Music. Here he discusses a speech by Julian Lloyd-Webber at the World Economic Forum in which Lloyd-Webber talked of 'the forty years of madness from 1945 to the early 80s'. In rejecting this kind of blue-rinse criticism, Kenyon is at pains to find some middle way between, on the one hand, a reactionary dismissal of the avant-garde and, on the other, an equally rabid manning of the barricades in its defence. What happened in the 1980s, Kenyon suggests, was:

> an acceptance that there wasn't a single way forward, that diversity was welcomed. It wasn't the death of the avant-garde. It was the absorption of the insights of the avant-garde onto a much broader musical canvas where they could co-exist with more tradi-tional elements and more far-off influences. It was the reintegration of contemporary music.[5]

Kenyon and Lloyd-Webber thus agree about the existence of climate change but disagree about its effects. Kenyon sees the flowering of wonderful hybrid forms that draw on the discoveries of the avant-garde but ameliorate these through more direct and communicative musical styles, while Lloyd-Webber hopes for the restoration of a normality in the climate that will promote abundant growth of tonal and melodic plants but see the freakish aberrations of the avant-garde wilt and disappear. Despite my lack of sympathy for the latter position, I think it should be taken seriously because it is far from being marginal or minority. Indeed, it is a fairly clear sub-text to a good deal of the apparently inclusive, all-comers-welcome, new-diversity speak.

Pluralism, in culture as in politics, is founded on the ideal of the coexistence of difference. It is an ideal that we would be ashamed to deny. And out of idealism – or political correctness – it is one whose products we seem to accept uncriti-cally. But the pluralist ideal presumes the coexistence of different positions without acknowledging the contradictions between them. At its worst, it rests on an extreme relativism which equals the absence of any values at all. The idea that anything goes equates, ultimately, to the idea that nothing matters. But to talk of culture at all presumes a collective sense of values (however contested and changeable) and to talk of art presumes judgement and (in the proper sense of the word) discrimination.

I suggest that the situation which I have been describing is far from the pluralist utopia that some of its advocates describe, that it is riven with contradictions which go unnoticed only because of a communal illiteracy with respect to music and a general confusion about the different claims and functions on which different musical styles are predicated. These considerations are far from abstract or theoretical: not only do they affect composers outwardly in their professional lives, they also impinge in subtle but specific ways on musical works themselves.

I want to make it clear that I am not suggesting that the coexistence of different musics is, in itself, problematic. That much is a central fact of contemporary life.

What is a cause for concern, however, is that this multiplication of cultural options seems, paradoxically, to be accompanied by a diminishing rather than expanding of musical imagination and thought. Potentially, these are exciting times. Today sees an unprecedented simultaneity of different stylistic options and gives composers enticing licence to move between different musical genres, even in the same piece. This contrasts strikingly, of course, with the language of high modernism, from Webern through Boulez, defined by a methodical exclusion of worldly elements (that is, popular and commercial materials). More recent music, with its emphasis on quotation, parody and stylistic montage may perhaps recall an earlier, pre-war version of modernism. And it is patently a healthy, even necessary, impulse for art that it should renew itself through contact with the heterogeneity of the real world, which for music may well mean engaging with the vernacular, as western art music has done periodically throughout its history. Witness composers as diverse as Stravinsky, Mahler, Haydn or Josquin.

Of course, these are controversial issues, but in the middle of such arguments it is salutary to imagine how our own time might be regarded in another hundred years. Perhaps we do live at a defining historical moment, in keeping with our precarious perch on the edge of a new millennium. But equally, 100 years on, perhaps the grand debates of modernity and postmodernity may seem no more than another *guerre des bouffons*, a storm in a stylistic teacup. It may be that at the close of this century we are witnessing a restoration of *two* kinds of musical practice which were definitive of musical modernism at the start of this century – a cultivation of both autonomous abstraction and an aesthetic wrestling with the heterogeneity of the world. And it may be that, in their coexistence, these two distinct modalities of modernism tell a truth about modern dilemmas to which neither one alone quite adds up.

This, I think, is not the real problem. Arguments about whether you should or should not create art music out of vernacular or old materials are sterile and pointless. Far more serious a problem – and one which gives real cause for concern – is the concomitant blurring and erosion of some fundamental aesthetic concepts. When Stravinsky or Haydn borrowed from popular dance forms, they did so in a cultural context in which the different functions of art music and the vernacular remained clearly demarcated. Today, when composers incorporate materials derived from vernacular and commercial music, they do so in a very different context. In their music the borrowing is an acknowledgement of a new social fact that, in purely social terms, aesthetic distinctions between musical types are increasingly irrelevant.

The lack of genuine and rigorous debate about these issues adds to a general confusion. Only extreme positions today afford their advocates a reassuring feeling of certainty – perhaps the one thing in common between the absolute relativist (all music is equally valuable) and the absolute partisan (only *this* music is valuable). For the rest of us, these are confusing times. There is a general sense that the ghettoization of new music in the second half of the twentieth century is a situation nobody wishes to continue, but there is far less agreement about how it is to be overcome. The buzzword of the 1990s was 'accessibility', much used in Arts Council discussion documents and by educationalists and concert promoters. In some contexts it referred simply to the breaking down of the unnecessary barriers surrounding classical and new music which put off a significant part of its potential audience, barriers arising from the exclusive cultural space in which this music is generally heard. But it is quite obviously also to do with musical language and style, by far the most significant reason for new music's small audience. This, of course, is a far more contentious question.

It is clear that organizers of contemporary music events increasingly feel able to offer a diversity of musical styles and languages in the same programme. It is also clear that composers themselves increasingly feel able to make use of a diversity of materials in their music, suggesting a loosening up of an earlier high-modernist position. What is far less clear is the relationship between these two things. The climate change model suggests that composers are now reflecting the changing conditions in which their music is made and heard. The eclectic pluralism of contemporary culture thus becomes a feature of musical works themselves.

This is by no means necessarily related to the question of 'accessibility'. A composer who uses elements of popular music does not immediately become more accessible if these elements are mediated and problematized as part of a wider musical discourse. By the same token, using rhythmic elements derived from popular music or harmonic elements derived from late-Romantic music does not necessarily confer on a composer the credentials of interesting, ironic, up-to-date postmodernist. Accessibility, at its best, suggests the communicability of great art; at its worst, it is a smokescreen for music that is simply bad. What is potentially harmful about its use today is the way it obscures a fundamental distinction between the concerns of art music and those of popular music.

If this distinction seems outmoded or even incomprehensible, that is perhaps an indication of a deeper change in the cultural climate of the late twentieth century. While plurality of musical style may be justly celebrated, the dominance of popular forms has tended to result in the application of its aesthetic as a yardstick for all musical types. Classical music has traditionally claimed a quite different function to that claimed by popular music, a difference which lies at the root of their different approach to musical material. Popular music is founded on an immediacy which art music tends to reject in favour of a critical and discursive engagement. This outward difference is rooted in the wider aspiration of art, not simply to *reproduce* the heterogeneity of the world, but to make sense of it by *transforming* it; to redeem the accidental nature of things by making them purposeful. It is not that art music wishes to be inaccessible, it is only that its more abstract, discursive engagement with musical material is necessarily less accessible than pure immediacy.

My point here is not to imply a criticism of either tradition, but to suggest that the confusion surrounding contemporary music arises from this deeper blurring of distinctions about musical function. In fact, so dominant is the function of popular music (that is, pleasure) that it is considered odd to raise the question of function at all. In this context classical music as a whole begins to change, as the Classic FM phenomenon demonstrates. The classical music that survives is increasingly those pockets and fragments which are able to fulfil the function of popular music. The same process has begun to impinge on contemporary music, a category which one might think is predicated on a refusal of the immediacy fundamental to popular music.

Perhaps this is why the multiplicity of today's musical world is both thrilling and enervating at the same time. It suggests the proliferation of difference but delivers a kind of flattening of the landscape. It is not that the music becomes all the same – far from it – but that all music becomes functionally equivalent. This is obvious in the marketing of the wide range of contemporary music, in its packaging on radio stations, in concert promotion and the marketing of performers and composers. It is even more obvious in the uniform rows of CDs in the Virgin Megastore. The equivalence of the CD (music as recorded object) is a perfect symbol for the flattening of functional distinctions which used to prevail between different musical types, and which constituted part of their difference and, therefore, value.

Some people will see these concerns as peripheral and will be exasperated by my avoidance of specific technical questions. But questions of function – of what music actually *does*, what it might be *for* – are the most fundamental of compositional questions and, ultimately, determine every technical decision. The question of 'How' one writes is inseparable from that of 'for Whom and Why'. What music is, what it says, what it does, is achieved only through the specific organization of specific materials. If music is more than an idle play with abstract patterns it is so because its materials and the patterning derived out of them are in some way socially and historically shaped, and in this way of social and historical significance.

This being the case, the materials and the forms with which a composer works are neither neutral nor arbitrary. Instead they define quite specific, if untranslatable, positions. These positions may be social, political, intellectual, emotional, psychological, theological ... even cosmological: they are metaphors like any other cultural forms for imagining and articulating human experience. In this context, compositional choices begin to take on rather a different aspect. Stating the matter clumsily but at least directly: to use different materials, to employ different musical processes, to arrive at different musical forms, is to say different things. Because these 'things' are untranslatable there is no simple or unequivocal definition of the position one adopts by writing in a certain way. But that does not mean that debate and contention, criticism and judgement are not possible and, if music matters at all, unresolvable debate seems preferable to the kind of hopelessly relativist, *laissez-faire* attitude which can no longer distinguish humane truths from utter inanity.

Musical material slips in and out of meaningfulness, in and out of meaningful tension and semantic richness in a way which we sense only dimly within our own time (though we are disdainful about those whom history has left beached for not spotting it in theirs). British music of the 1990s exhibits a very wide range of responses to the musical materials which make up the sound world of contemporary culture, from the autonomous linguistic concerns of high modernism to an overt engagement with the materials of other musical traditions. There are signs here of an exciting shake-up that may help redress a balance, lost in some post-war music, between formal coherence and heterogeneous material, between the concrete sound and the abstract idea, without which art has no productive tension. But in this shake-up we should keep our critical faculties sharp. The multiple musical choices we are offered do not constitute equivalent answers to the questions with which music deals.

The idea of an art music rests upon a primary concern with musical language and with the demands it seems to make upon composer and listener alike. While we may still understand very little about the way in which musical language is shaped by historical culture, every composer knows from first-hand experience that musical materials exert their own demands and allow only compositional solutions that realize those demands. It is this attitude to musical material that lies at the basis of the apparent 'difficulties' not only of contemporary music, but of Bach or Beethoven for that matter. If all musical materials are today equally possible (ancient and modern, western and non-western, art and pop) they are by no means equally meaningful. The fact that the rules governing musical semantics are elusive to codification does not mean that everything and anything works: it is possible to write music that is, strictly speaking, nonsense. It is possible that it might be extremely well received, praised for its accessibility and valued in direct proportion to its popularity.

Cultural plurality offers exciting new possibilities. But if we are to distinguish between genuinely new formulations and nonsense we need a more self-critical and self-reflexive attitude rather than the opposite. There is nothing politically correct about the loss of one's ability to distinguish between the two in a culture which values style over discourse, material over form, immediacy of surface over the idea. Not all musical choices are equally valid, and while the liberating gain of own time may well be a reaffirmation of the idea that in art there is always more than one right answer, we should counter with passion the proliferation of those that are objectively nonsense and literally untrue.

Notes

1   Beverley Crew, 'Now that is what I call "contemporary"!', *new notes* (January 1999), p. 1.
2   Shortly after I gave the paper on which this article is based, Beverley Crew's piece was

discussed by Roger Redgate in the April 1999 edition of *new notes*. A reply from Beverley Crew was printed in the May edition.

3   Joby Talbot, 'Keeping busy ...', *new notes* (February 1999), p. 1.
4   Joanna MacGregor, 'Plugging in ...', *new notes* (December 1998), p. 2.
5   Nicholas Kenyon, '1940s to 80s: Forty years of madness?', *new notes* (December 1998), p. 1.

Chapter 3

The Artists' Dilemma

Edwin Roxburgh

After a lifetime of performing, composing and thinking about music, I find myself asking the question: why am I troubled? It struck me recently while I was reading an interview with Boulez by Rob Cowan in *The Independent* entitled 'Voulez-vous Boulez?', and sub-headed 'modernist *bête-noire* or champion of the new?'[1] The interview itself was intelligent and informative, and thus ill-served by the phrases I have quoted, suggestive of a polarizing of attitudes wholly unrepresentative of the subtle arguments of the interview itself. While 'Voulez-vous Boulez?' defies comment, the presumption that modernism is a territory inhabited by aliens is obfuscation taken to its limits. I say obfuscation, because labelling is a mere convenience for identification rather than an explanation of individual qualities. To confuse the two, as some historians frequently do, simply creates a false impression. The idea that you can only be a composer if you join a labelled school certainly makes things neat and tidy for commentators, but it says nothing about the individuality which is essential for true creativity. For instance, no three composers are more distinctive than the so-called Second Viennese School of Schoenberg, Berg and Webern, yet their historical epitaph is chiselled in stone. I go further, and maintain that the music of no substantial composer in history or today can be qualified by the tenets of a fashionable cult. Couperin defended his distinctiveness in copious prefaces. J.S. Bach was seen as an old-fashioned fuddy-duddy during his life but he is timeless in his eternal monumentality. Mozart avoided the *galant* style almost completely, but stands as a monument to its age.

Today's version of cult identification is seen in the application of information theory; the soundbite, the bullet-point comment, the quick reference on the website, the result of which is a minimalist approach towards explaining the essence of any subject. You cannot compose poetry in shorthand, and composers who can wear a label without protest tend to produce weak, prescriptive music. The danger of information theory (as distinct from technology) is that it subjugates the individual to a system which relegates substance to a level of secondary importance. This impinges on the systems which funding bodies are compelled to employ, in that prescriptive conditions are imposed which sometimes work against their best intentions. Simon Rattle puts it: 'We spend our time jumping through hoops trying to prove our right to exist at all.'[2] Thus the financing of Music Education projects is governed by constraints, which result in a situation where, despite the potential benefits of contact with leading composers, young people are encouraged in the belief that improvising with basic sounds is composing. The obfuscation is sustained by many areas of the commercial world of music, with its tendency to trivialize art: quality is inevitably sacrificed to popular appeal. The system has a carefully constructed defence against attack, and any attempt to address this state of affairs is to invite the label 'elitist', with the art of composition itself on the pillory. Perhaps the saddest aspect of the current situation is that so many good musicians have to acquiesce in the empty rhetoric of this information world.

To return to subsidy. Even Genghis Khan recognized that art cannot exist if the artist starves to death. He certainly subsidized art, even if it was for self-aggrandizement. The need for subsidy is even more imperative today, and composers are often the victims of injustice in this respect. It is offensive to hear, from sources close to government, that composers are 'elitist and arrogant', and that 'they think the world owes them a living'. The truth is that most composers (like myself) earn much of their living with their supporting skills, which, if they think as I do, stimulated their creative abilities. But this does not mean that their enterprises can be self-financed: art projects have to be subsidized or they cannot exist. This is not, as some would claim, a situation unique to our time. It is significant that when Rossini visited Beethoven in 1822, *The Barber of Seville* had received over 100 performances, while *Fidelio*, after a successful revival in 1814, languished in comparative obscurity. Beethoven's music was not just 'out of fashion', but was not understood, and his last quartets were scarcely performed during the years after his death. Half a century later, they were dismissed by as substantial a figure as Tchaikovsky, and this in spite of his own not inconsiderable contributions to the genre. In fact, there has never been a commercial guarantee for art of great depth, and the situation is exacerbated in today's quick-fix world. Yes, it *is* because art is essentially elitist that it cannot put popular appeal before artistic integrity. Only people who have developed a cultured interest in art can judge such qualities. *That* is elitism, and I defend it.

While most large conglomerates limit their subsidies to traditional concerts for sure-fire returns, the smaller private funding bodies attached to composers' names such as Ralph Vaughan Williams, Holst, Tippett, Britten, together with the Hinrichsen Foundation, sustain their heart-warming loyalty with discrimination and keen judgement of the art of music they support and sponsor. Looking back over the years in which the Arts Council has been in operation, we can recognize Arts Ministers of differing political allegiances who performed wonderfully, simply because they loved art. They were heady days when Jenny Lee sat in front of the Treasury door with Lord Goodman until the £30 million she was demanding for the Arts was granted. In more recent times, the ones who really understood, like Norman St John-Stevas and David Mellor, sadly lost their jobs before they could be effective. Composers are unanimous in praising the caring supervision over so many years of John Cruft, whose work ensured the availability of commission fees for composers of all types throughout his reign, as well as initiating the Contemporary Music Network. While recognizing that the kind of bureaucracy which has now enveloped such organizations must be difficult for administrators to cope with, the musical world abounds with rumours that further changes are in the air, which will limit financial resources even more than in recent times. Let us hope that our fears are unjustified. After all, our two London-based opera companies have survived as a result of Richard Eyres reversing the recommendation of Sir Denis Stephenson's report to amalgamate English National Opera and Covent Garden. Mergers might work in business: in the Arts they are poison. The artist was heeded on this occasion and rescued two of our finest institutions.

The recent Tooley report on music conservatoires listed nine members on its panel, only two of whom were performers, and one of those, Sarah Walker, resigned within months. Perhaps that is why paragraph 16 of the summary of conclusions reads as follows: 'There is a national shortage of instrumental teachers of quality, and yet the matter is neglected as a field of national policy. A national examination of arrangements for training and teaching of performance should be instituted ...'.[3]

'A shortage of instrumental teachers of quality'? Before Sir Keith Joseph initiated the ending of free peripatetic teaching of musical instruments in schools, following the advent of the Thatcher government in 1979, we enjoyed a renaissance (a word often used in the preceding decade), which was intrinsically linked with the high quality of this teaching throughout the country. Those fine teachers still exist, but many of them are without jobs in schools. What has replaced them? While some lucky youngsters still learn music through an instrument, the accent is now on what is described as creative work in the classroom. Composers have replaced the peripatetics and are described as *animateurs* – it sounds less vacuous in French! The projects they animate might serve quite well as an imaginative exploration of basic sound, but the intellectual process of comprehending the substance of music is bypassed, the events soon forgotten by children because they learn nothing about the subject. Music can only be learned by a mature representation of its substance in a composed work of art. I consider it to be both demeaning and patronizing to ask children to treat composition as a game. I say patronizing because children are very adept at dealing with, for instance, the complexities of computers. Learning the rudiments of notation is, by comparison, a straightforward task, especially if it is directly related to the sounds of a scale-based instrument. Guido d'Arezzo's codification of notational principles arose from the need to provide a discipline for the music-making of recalcitrant choirboys: the development of western music over the centuries might well have been less fruitful if he had not asserted an educational approach towards helping these youngsters to understand music. Banging and strumming is fun, but it rarely aspires to structural organization even on an elementary level.

The defence against such criticism is often voiced with the use of words such as 'relevance' and 'accessibility'. Culture has to be 'relevant' and 'accessible' to conform to the ideals of dumbing down. Investing music with a 1990s relevance has made 'accessibility' come to mean 'for the uncultured'. This reluctance to challenge the intellectual and imaginative faculties stultifies the potential of young people to respond to the subtleties of art music, and their capacity to be transformed by its eloquence. The assumption that a 'project' should simply harness their untutored abilities ignores the fact that they have the capacity both to cope with the demands of musical notation and to develop a critical faculty in relation to the own creative efforts. Not to acknowledge this is tantamount to a belief that the majority of people are incapable of experiencing music on any but the most primitive of levels. Making culture 'accessible' makes it less possible for people to gain access to profound works of art. The result of this sad state of affairs is reflected in a recent MORI study, which found that: 'In only 27% of schools is demand for instrumental/vocal music tuition being fully met.'[4] It also found that the number of orchestras, bands and music groups was down. Only 55% of schools said they had an orchestra, down from 66% five years ago. The number of wind bands and recorder groups has also slumped.[5] The fact that secondary schools are offering more electric guitar than piano lessons is indicative of the trend towards displacing classical music with a pop culture in schools. Sir Paul McCartney does not, by his own admission, read music, yet is able to equate his harmonic vocabulary with that of Monteverdi. It is sad, because McCartney's contribution to his own genre is unequivocally great: nonetheless, an incomprehension towards art music pervades the culture of the pop world. The appearance of a photo of Stockhausen on the sleeve of the Beatles' cult *Sergeant Pepper* album only serves to emphasize the point. Superficial similarities there may be between the sound world of electro-acoustic music and moments in the Beatles' album, but there the comparison (at least in musical terms) is at end. The awesome technical command of the craft of composition and the complexity of musical structure exhibited in the music of Stockhausen places it in a different world from that of pop music, with its essentially commercial concerns. This does not imply that there is a sharp division between the two cultures, but simply that the vocabulary of pop music is colloquial and comparatively undeveloped in comparison to that of art music. I repeat that, for this reason, one culture should not displace the other.

The art of music requires structured education like any other subject. The recent government decision to double the level of funding to music in schools will be of no value unless we raise the status of the subject to the level of the 1960s. The huge gap between GCSE and A level requirements is indicative of the problem, and the solution lies not in compromising the standards of the latter. Rather it is the early training curriculum which needs to address the matter of musical literacy, otherwise the increases in resourcing for music will have been to no avail. This was well illustrated in Clare Fox's speech at the 1998 Edinburgh

Book Festival: 'When teachers look to students for relevance, and students have nothing profound to look to teachers for, the tendency is to mind-numbing stasis. The tyranny of relevance can lead only to a culture of *Teletubbies* for adults'.[6]

I have not drawn these conclusions simply as an armchair critic. Because I am a composer I consider it my duty, indeed my obsession, to protect this wonderful art form. For that reason I optimistically involved myself in the very arena I castigate in the attempt to change the collision course of a doomed ship. I believe in trying to make a positive situation out of a negative one. I called it the *Galileo* project. It took the form of a major symphonic work for chorus and electronics, in celebration of the millennium. Its subject was the marriage of music and science through Galileo the astronomer (The Harmony of the Spheres), and the 1990 space probe of the same name, with the potential musical benefits deriving indirectly from its technological achievements. The pilot scheme was in the form of an education programme financed by the Arts Council. I had the good fortune to work with an excellent *animateur* – although I would prefer to revert to the more traditional title of 'teacher'. Robert Jarvis developed my subject into an educational project which co-ordinated a programme of study based on the Galileo themes of music, science and technology. With the recorded results at my disposal I transformed the childrens' recordings into a through-composed composition with live instrumental performers and electronics. All this (and more) was presented with the collaboration of the staff of the London Planetarium in wonderful digi-star projections at the Planetarium, with musicians from the London Festival Orchestra providing the instrumental contribution. The education aspect of this project attempted to reinstate the early study of music as an integral aspect of creative thought and its links with the imaginative world of poetry, literature, history and physics. Building a bridge into this territory cannot be achieved in one attempt, but I hope the course set has led some young people to a land of self-discovery and cultural enrichment. I wish it could be followed through with training in the basic musical theory which would help them articulate even better musical ideas.

The first complete performance of *Galileo* took place at the Royal Festival Hall in September 2000. The music produced by pupils of Lambeth schools formed two distinctive interludes between the three movements of the work. These tableaux were co-ordinated by Avril and David Sutton-Anderson, and the electro-acoustic elements supervised by Michael Oliva, who took the children beyond the scope of classroom keyboards in the deployment of sophisticated electronic techniques. This was especially significant in that some of the original compositions, presented in an introductory concert before the main orchestral event, demonstrated a creative and imaginative use of technology. The incorporation of children and their music within the vast dimensions of the oratorio *Galileo* gave them the experience of listening to a large orchestra, chorus and baritone soloist, while preparing for their own contribution in the two interludes. The inclusion of a children's ripieno chorus in the oratorio itself enhanced this

integration of young people within a professional context. The London Festival
Orchestra, conducted by Ross Pople (who inaugurated the project), was the sound
source for the elaboration of live electronic treatments at the first performance,
and the technician thus assumed the role of orchestral technician.

In the three movements of *Galileo*, the electronic element is deployed as an
aspect of the age-old marriage of music and science from Pythagoras onwards.
This relationship has been the foundation for the evolution of musical language
through plainchant, modal, tonal and post-tonal eras, underlining the importance
of acoustic science in the creative process. IRCAM has become a model for
studios in cities and educational institutions across the world, and in this context,
Galileo is a statement on the history of the science–music marriage in which
music can be seen as a creative product of scientific motivation. J.S. Bach made
such a statement in the '48', that comprehensive demonstration of the poten-
tialities of the then new system of tempered tuning. In doing so, he created an
unsurpassable monument to the universality of musical substance. Music, like
people, does not change in nature from one era to another, only in idiom and style.

Galileo was my chosen subject for many reasons, the most important being that
this great seventeenth-century physicist, whose father was a composer, represents
the opening of the frontiers of science after 1500 years of Aristotelian rule. By
turning his telescope towards the stars (having produced a lens capable of magni-
fication by a thousandfold) and identifying the four moons of Jupiter, the heavens
opened to disclose a boundless universe which created imaginative notions about
the relationship between the harmonic series of musical sound and its possible
geometric relationships in the orbits of the planets. Faulty though it was, this
concept of 'the harmony of the spheres' was reflected in the literature and science
of the time. The first movement of my oratorio, 'The Man', explores this beautiful
world with a baritone soloist in the guise of Galileo himself, singing a rhapsody
of literary and scientific writings. Milton asks us to 'Listen to the Celestial Sirens'
Harmony', while the scientist Brunel tells us he can 'cut the heavens and rise to
the infinite'. Shakespeare's 'touches of sweet harmony' relates to the 'spheres',
and additional material by the composer gives a strong identity to the singer as
Galileo, but not without a short reference to Pascal's 'infinite spaces'. Without
resorting to pastiche, the music is inlaid with a motet by Lassus, *O vos omnes*,
which evokes a renaissance spirit, but triggers the composer's essentially twenty-
first century spirit and idiom.

The second movement, 'The Mission', takes us to the 'Galileo' Space Mission
of the twentieth century. Space research at the National Aeronautics and Space
Administration (NASA) has evolved most of the computer technology which now
dominates our society, and in turn provides the equipment for electro-acoustic
music. Sadly, this century of incredible scientific evolution has been dominated
by some of the worst atrocities in the history of the world. For this reason, the
movement is a lament for the victims of conflict. The second tableau relates to the
modern age of space travel. Emerging from this, student participants from the

education project form a procession leading to the platform, singing music which introduces the theme of the final movement, 'The Future'. Electronic treatments enhance their song, culminating at last in the children's ripieno choir repeating it in the context of the final movement. A female chorus uses words by E.E. Cummings ('these children singing') to create cascading canons over electronic fusions. The baritone soloist emerges from this with a universal statement drawn from a poem by Boethius, *Si vis celsi iura tonantis*. The second orchestral commentary leads to a final chorus, drawing together all the musical elements, again set to words by Cummings, 'hope, faith!', in a vast orchestral carillon – a veritable 'fanfare for the future'.

The millennium marked the culmination of a century of great diversity in the arts. It is a diversity which we should celebrate – but not without discrimination. Bernard Shaw and Oscar Wilde threw plenty of boulders at dumbing-down trends in the 1890s, and it may well be that the stuff of history can only be carried on a ballast of mediocrity. In the Boulez interview which I cited at the beginning of this chapter, he summed up the matter when he said that 'people have become lazy' but that 'we must not be discouraged by this lack of energy'. He stated his belief that 'the pendulum will swing back'. Let us hope that it will not be too long in returning, because there is plenty of evidence of this inertia in today's preoccu-pation with minimalism by so many lazy composers. They do not wish to disturb people or to seek the challenges of invention. 'Reaching out' is a phrase which many minimalists *also* tend to use to describe their patronization of mass audi-ences. The capacity houses for concerts centred on the music of Boulez proves that they misjudge the receptivity of audiences to innovation. The lethargy mentioned by Boulez actually comes from the agencies and commercial adminis-trators who have a vested interest in tradition, and a monopoly on the propagation of art. Innovation is a threat to their laboriously constructed world.

The added problem for musicians today is that in a consumer society they are judged by financial returns and box office. Opportunities for the performance of large-scale works are minimal. With the exception of the BBC orchestras, most London-based and provincial symphony orchestras present a very small pro-portion of the vast repertoire available to them, very often repeating similar programmes again and again in what they believe to be the only way to guarantee the audiences and sums needed to sustain themselves. Ten years ago, they entered the educational field, as I have discussed. While the musicians have given their artistry with zeal and sincerity, Arts Council research has revealed that the primary objective of orchestras in educational projects is to achieve larger audi-ences and to gain the extra funding involved: truly educational motives were not very prominent. There is not much room for composers in such a scenario. As functional musicians we have our arsenals in organizations such as the Society for the Promotion of New Music, the BBC, the Park Lane Group, performing ensembles, and our universities and colleges. But it is also imperative for us to uphold the aspirational character of our art at a fundamental level in schools, to help those teachers who work so hard for love of music and for its intelligent propagation against a tide of ignorance.

Those charged with the responsibility for the distribution of funds would do well to heed the words of Browning in his poem, *Abt Vogler*:

> But God has a few of us whom he whispers in the ear:
> The rest may reason and welcome: 'tis we musicians know.

Notes

1   *The Independent*, 26 January 1999.
2   *The Independent*, 21 December 1998.
3   Higher Education Funding Council for England, Report 98/11, 'Review of Music Conservatoires', HEFCE Conservatoires Advisory Group chaired by Sir John Tooley, March 1998.
4   Performing Right Society in conjunction with PricewaterhouseCoopers and MORI, Musical Instrument Tuition in Schools, PRS, February 1999, p. 2. 7.
5   Ibid., p. 8.
6   Reproduced as 'Podium: British Culture is Dumbing Down', *The Independent*, 25 August 1998.

Chapter 4

In the Shadows of Song: Birtwistle's Nine Movements for String Quartet

Robert Adlington

Birtwistle's Nine Movements for String Quartet have a complicated compositional history. They emerged, not as a single incorporated work, but piecemeal over a period of five years, in response to various different commissions.[1] Their identity as a cycle has additionally been blurred by their eventual combination with Birtwistle's settings of the poetry of Paul Celan, under the collective title *Pulse Shadows*. It was in this form that the quartet movements received their first complete performance in April 1996. The Celan settings themselves emerged in a similarly protracted manner. Figure 4.1 summarizes the complex evolution of both cycles.

In his second book on Birtwistle, Michael Hall compares the alternation of songs and quartets in *Pulse Shadows* with the similarly interleaved arrangement of vocal and instrumental movements in *Le marteau sans maître*, and quotes Birtwistle as saying that the two combined cycles form 'two parallel sequences of music ... one being a comment on the other'.[2] The parallel with Boulez's work is heightened, arguably, by the fact that the nine quartet movements are themselves divided into 'Friezes' and 'Fantasias', meaning that overall there is some resemblance to the tripartite arrangement of *Le marteau*.[3] However, as the history of the cycle's composition suggests, *Pulse Shadows* possesses little of the structural integration of *Le marteau*. Birtwistle freely admits that the work was the product

1989   'White and Light'
1991   Movement for String Quartet   [Frieze 1]
1992   Three Settings of Celan ('White and Light', 'Tenebrae', 'Night')
1993   Three Movements for String Quartet [Frieze 1, Fantasia 2, Fantasia 4]
1994   'With Letter and Clock'
1995   'Todtnauberg'
1996   'An Eye, Open'
1996   *Pulse Shadows* [Nine Movements for String Quartet and Nine Settings of Celan]

Figure 4.1   *Pulse Shadows*

of a chain of accidents,[4] and it is consistent with this that the printed score should allow for the work to be performed 'either complete or in part'. In this chapter I wish to expand on the question of coherence as it relates specifically to the quartet movements. In particular, I am concerned to separate the genuine kinships that exist between individual movements from the mythical ones that have sometimes been presumed by writers on Birtwistle's music. I will also propose some connections that can be drawn between the quartet movements and other works by Birtwistle. It may be thought unremarkable that such connections should exist, but in fact in important respects these pieces appear somewhat at odds with Birtwistle's more customary preoccupations. This observation forms the starting point for my discussion.

At the first British performance of *Pulse Shadows*, it was perhaps inevitable that attention should focus more upon the Celan settings than upon the quartet movements.[5] The Celan texts, for all their difficulty as poetry, provided an element of ready comprehensibility which the quartets seemed not to possess; and this impression was reinforced by a specially conceived staging which placed the singer centre stage and consigned the quartet to the side – not an equal partner at all. The relative inscrutability of the quartet movements cannot simply be explained by their lack of a text, however, or an unfavourable stage placing. These quartet pieces can be understood to exist in the 'shadows' of song in other, more intrinsic ways. They are, for one thing, notably lacking in sustained melody. As Michael Hall has noted, whereas 'the songs are essentially lyrical and depend on "melodic development", the quartet pieces are based on "rhythmic development"'.[6] This places them closer in style to the percussive toccatas of *Harrison's Clocks* for piano (1997), than to the Celan settings. We are largely denied, in the quartet movements, the linear thread that so often sees us through Birtwistle's otherwise frequently inhospitable landscapes.[7]

Birtwistle's choice of medium is also significant. The string quartet is essentially an homogeneous ensemble and does not immediately suggest options for instrumental drama. One might make a comparison with the wind quintet, which Birtwistle uses in *Refrains and Choruses* and *Five Distances*. There the horn is something of an 'odd man out', by virtue of its contrasting appearance and construction. The string quartet provides considerably less basis for such differentiation. Indeed, it is the ensemble that, perhaps more than any other, sets into high relief what Fred Maus has called 'a pervasive *indeterminacy* in the identification of musical agents'.[8] In the classical quartet repertoire, one instrument (typically the first violin) may on occasion strike out alone, so that its part seems to correspond (in the words of Maus) 'to the activity of a single agent, determinately set apart from the rest of the ensemble'. Elsewhere, however, as Maus says, 'it seems appropriate to think of the *whole texture* of a piece as the action of a single agent'.[9] In listening to a classical quartet, we are often required to alternate rapidly between these different 'schemes of individuation':[10] a musical persona may be conjured up by a single instrument at one moment, the whole ensemble at the next. In other words, instrumental roles are not fixed. This presents a challenge to any composer concerned to project some sort of instrumental theatre. To override the indeterminacy of musical agency in the quartet requires a particularly concerted effort – of the sort found in Elliott Carter's String Quartet No. 2, where the four instrumentalists are instructed to sit as far apart from each other as possible, in order to emphasize their distinctness as characters. Birtwistle's Movements adopt no such strategies, and they seem largely content to leave instrumental role-play out of the equation. There are sporadic exceptions: principally, the viola takes a prominent role, albeit fleetingly, in three of the nine movements. But in general the music's progress does not appear to be governed or explained by such roles – in contrast to many of Birtwistle's other instrumental works.

So the Movements seem distant from two prominent, characteristic elements of Birtwistle's music: melody and instrumental drama. It would be incorrect, however, to give the impression that they are quite unconnected with the rest of Birtwistle's output. Several such connections will be remarked upon in the course of this article. One particularly obvious association concerns the cycle's allusion to the idea of the musical 'frieze'. Four of the nine movements are entitled 'Frieze' (see Figure 4.2), and this echoes the title of a work for large ensemble completed shortly before *Pulse Shadows*, *Slow Frieze*.[11] In an interview given in early 1996 – which is to say, at about the same time as both *Pulse Shadows* and *Slow Frieze* were brought to completion – Birtwistle offered the following explanation for the significance of this term for his music: 'the idea of a frieze in music is something central to my work – that is, it explains itself in blocks of musical material, and these blocks can return in various guises.'[12] Here Birtwistle is proposing that the frieze can be understood as an analogy for his sectional (or 'block') forms. The parallel is particularly clear if one thinks of the Doric friezes that adorn the buildings of ancient Greece. This type of frieze takes the form of a succession of enclosed panels, so that, to quote Elma Sanders, 'the visual effect ... is one of repeated structural modules'.[13] *Slow Frieze* is likewise constructed from

i	Fantasia 1
ii	Frieze 1
iii	Fantasia 2
iv	Fantasia 3
v	Frieze 2
vi	Fantasia 4
vii	Frieze 3
viii	Fantasia 5
ix	Todesfuge-Frieze 4

Figure 4.2   Nine Movements for String Quartet

sections of contrasting material, which are often juxtaposed quite abruptly. Indeed, this approach to form is characteristic of Birtwistle's larger works generally.

Pulse Shadows, or for that matter the cycle of quartet movements by themselves, can be viewed in a similar way. There is of course one significant difference: these cycles comprise a number of separate pieces rather than a single extended one. But according to at least one commentator, all the constituent parts or modules in *Pulse Shadows* 'share the same spiritual terrain';[14] the dovetailing of several of the movements emphasizes this sense of a shared common concern. That *Pulse Shadows* may justifiably be conceived as a single, large, sectional form, is confirmed by Birtwistle's own comparison with the verse structures of earlier works. Birtwistle proposes that 'the string quartets and the songs in *Pulse Shadows* ... are both functioning as the ritornello to the other, simultaneously ... There's an element [of identical repetition], in that one is being played by a string quartet without a song, and then the other has a voice and it's a different instrumentation'.[15] This situation, where two or more types of distinct material are deployed in alternation, may be found in many of Birtwistle's pieces from the 1960s onwards. Rather than opt for a literal verse and refrain scheme, in which a repeating element (the refrain) is interspersed between a changing element (the different verses), Birtwistle typically brings back *all* his material in altered form, so that it is difficult to make an absolute distinction between verse and refrain. In *Pulse Shadows*, the alternation of two distinct instrumental groups whose successive contributions comprise different pieces, does indeed broadly adhere to the same scheme, as Birtwistle suggests.

Birtwistle likes to stress the continuities between his different pieces, and it is hard to dispute the similarities in design that he identifies. Nevertheless, his comparison here risks ascribing greater cogency to *Pulse Shadows* than it actually possesses. The disparate composition dates of the individual pieces, and the flexibility that allows parts of the cycle to be extracted, have already been noted. *Pulse Shadows* hardly amounts to a single, composite sectional form in the way that, for instance, *Verses for Ensembles* or *Carmen Arcadiae Mechanicae Perpetuum* do.

There is, however, another, rather different way to understand the analogy of the frieze in relation to these pieces. It is one that is less dependent on the modular, panelled structure typical of the Doric frieze. Later Greek architecture, for instance, 'employed a frieze filled with a *continuous* band of figured relief sculpture ... The visual effect of an Ionic frieze is one of uninterrupted horizontality.'[16] This second sort of frieze makes particularly apparent a tension present in any sculptural form, between the sculpture's static, immobile qualities and the element of temporality or motion that is required in order properly to view it. The tension is particularly marked when the sculpture takes the form of a horizontal band. Large friezes of this sort obligate the viewer to move around a room or building (or at the very least require a pronounced turning of the head) in order to perceive the whole. As such, they make manifest a temporal element present in the perception of *all* visual art, but which is more usually confined to the rapid flitting of the eye. Both *Slow Frieze* and the quartet pieces play as much on this aspect of the frieze, as on the modular one. *Slow Frieze* features a musical analogy for the frieze's paradoxical 'mobile staticity' in the form of an 'unchanging harmonic backdrop'[17] that appears periodically in the wind instruments. This backdrop is created by weaving, melodic lines which, taken together, spell out fixed harmonic fields. The music moves, and yet stays still. The four quartet movements entitled 'Frieze' possess a similarly marked quality of mobile staticity, though they achieve it through different means. These will be discussed further below.

In the Nine Movements Birtwistle interleaves his four Friezes with five 'Fantasias', an arrangement that creates a further layer of verse-like alternations when the cycle is performed in its entirety. The intended distinction is an obvious one: the granitic formality of the frieze presents a contrast to the greater freedom and fluidity of the fantasia. Once again though, the larger-scale pattern suggested by the movements' titles needs to be viewed with some caution. Michael Hall has revealed that the word 'freeze' (spelt with two 'e's) appears in the sketches for the very first quartet movement, and concludes from this that the idea of the musical frieze was present from the very earliest stage in the cycle's evolution.[18] But although this movement was eventually to become the completed cycle's Frieze 1, the word 'Frieze' did not appear in the 1991 score; nor did it – or its eventual counterpart 'Fantasia' – feature in the published score of the Three Movements for String Quartet (these movements eventually became Fantasia 2, Fantasia 4 and Frieze 1 of the Nine Movements). The composer's own note (written in 1993) to the Three Movements mentions neither title, and fails to remark upon any significant disparity between the first two pieces and the third. Even in early 1996, as the remaining quartet movements were becoming available from Boosey & Hawkes, they were labelled simply with numbers, according to the order of composition.[19] It was only with the penultimate movement to be written, the 'Todesfuge', that the additional title 'Frieze 4' appeared. There is ample material evidence, then, for treating the titles as a relatively casual unifying device, thought up at a very late stage in the cycle's composition and of limited relevance to the actual music. Arnold Whittall has even proposed that 'Birtwistle has chosen two different titles simply to highlight ... the arbitrariness of attempted distinctions between them ... The implied generic dialectic between frieze and fantasia turns out to be a stimulus for music which actually throws that dialectic into doubt ...'.[20] This is perhaps too sceptical a viewpoint. In fact, the opposition of strict and free *is* loosely borne out in the individual pieces. Each of the Friezes is notable for adhering to a broadly consistent type of material for its entire duration, a pattern that culminates in the quasi-fugal structure of Frieze 4, which was written in response to Celan's famous poem, 'Todesfuge'. The Fantasias, on the other hand, progress more fitfully; they each contain a number of discrete and contrasted

sections, and incorporate greater differentiation in the treatment of the four instruments. So the Nine Movements do fall into distinguishable *types*. But it should
not be presumed that these types are comprehensively accounted for in terms of
the two titles that Birtwistle appended to the final printed score.

In elaborating upon these types of movement – the kinships within the cycle –
I want first to focus upon the five Fantasias. Appropriately, given their title, they
all give considerable room for individual instruments to make themselves heard.
But they do this in two different ways. In fact, it is possible to discern two
mini-cycles within the Fantasias: Fantasias 1 and 2 share important characteristics, and so do Fantasias 3, 4 and 5. Fantasias 1 and 2 both fall into two distinct
halves, and solo instruments come to the fore in the second half of each piece.
These two second halves are strikingly similar to each other. They both comprise
a long succession of unison chords, each chord separated by rests; into these
successions of chords are interjected brief but more rhetorical figures from individual instruments. An idea of the characteristic texture of the second parts of
Fantasias 1 and 2 respectively is given in Example 4.1. The first halves of these
two fantasias, on the other hand, are very different from each other. Fantasia 1,
the seventh of the pieces to be written, seems to acknowledge its eventual role as
the opening piece of the completed cycle, for it is dominated by extremely aggressive, attention-grabbing double-stopping. Birtwistle has likened this opening to the
beginning of Monteverdi's Vespers,[21] and it does indeed comprise a sort of static
fanfare. The first half of Fantasia 2 is gentler and structurally more complex. As
Birtwistle notes, it 'begins three times';[22] in between the second and third of these
'beginnings' appear anticipations both of the movement's chordal second half
and its temporally unsynchronized coda.

Fantasias 3, 4 and 5 focus on the individual voice of the viola, and take a rather
more improvisatory form. Each of these movements is also preoccupied with a
particular rhythmic idea – comprising a sustained, double-stopped chord which is
preceded by a brief 'upbeat' and followed by a staccato note.[23] Examples of this
motive are given in Example 4.2. In each case it forms a steady, gentle foil to
passages of frenetic viola activity. The viola's soloistic efforts meet different fates
in each piece. Fantasia 5 opens with a nervous demisemiquaver pattern played
imitatively by all the instruments, but the viola wriggles free of this restrictive
texture. It then progressively increases its individuality to the extent that it eventually takes leave of the main tempo. In Fantasia 4, the wayward viola is several
times savagely halted by unison chords from the other instruments. In Fantasia 3,
on the other hand, it seems to be met simply with a weary tolerance. Fantasia 3,
incidentally, was the last of the nine movements to be completed, and it is difficult
not to see it as a hasty addition to the set, rather than a necessary and distinct
component. It is by far the shortest of the Nine Movements, and is essentially a
pale summary of the more vividly dramatic Fantasia 4.

Ironically, the sectionality of most of the Fantasias finds little reflection in
the Friezes, even though (as has been discussed) the title 'frieze' might lead one

**Example 4.1   Harrison Birtwistle, characteristic texture of second half of
Fantasias 1 and 2**

to expect the opposite. Only one of the Friezes falls into clearly defined
sections. This is Frieze 1, the earliest of the quartet movements, which was
written in 1991 as a self-contained birthday tribute to Alfred Schlee. It remains
at one remove from the other pieces. Its juxtaposition of melody and rhythmic
material is entirely characteristic of other works of the late 1980s and very early
1990s, but makes for a contrast with the predominantly non-melodic quality of
the rest of the cycle. Despite its differences, Frieze 1 is consistent with the other
Friezes in largely adhering to the same material for the piece's entire length. It
explores a variety of ways of deploying its two contrasting elements (namely a
rather nervous, accented 'cantus' line, and scurrying, semiquaver-based

Fantasia 2

Example 4.1   continued

rhythmic patterns) between the four instruments; the turning point seems to come when the cello finally wrests the melody for itself, having previously been consigned to rather anonymous ostinato and pulse patterns. Thereafter the music's distinct elements dissolve, violin 1 and cello drifting outwards to their registral extremes.

According to Michael Hall, the sketches for Frieze 1 reveal that the open strings of the violins and viola formed one of Birtwistle's points of departure: they become pivotal pitches for the scurrying semiquaver patterns that are one of the work's primary components.[24] Frieze 1 is not the only Movement to give a

Example 4.2   Harrison Birtwistle, characteristic rhythmic idea in Fantasias 3, 4 and 5

prominent role to open strings. They are indeed unusually evident throughout the cycle, particularly in the numerous passages of double-stopping. As Birtwistle notes in the interview accompanying this article, this strategy makes such passages somewhat easier to play. That said, the performers' convenience hardly seems to be an overriding criterion in this music, and the significance of the open strings is perhaps better understood in terms of their distinctive sound quality. A passage towards the end of Fantasia 4 goes further still in making *the instruments themselves* part of the musical equation: its languid string-crossing bears more than a passing resemblance to the process of tuning up (Example 4.3). Permitting the mechanics of an instrument to determine aspects of compositional structure is hardly a characteristic strategy of post-war musical modernism, which has more often seemed intent on treating all instruments as neutral media for the transmission of abstractly conceived pitch formations. But this is not the first time that it has happened in Birtwistle's music. The early *Monody for Corpus Christi* bares the traces of the Holst songs for voice and violin that inspired it, in the form of the four pitches of the violin's open strings, which are made prominent in all four parts throughout the piece. Further studies of the sketches for the Nine Movements may help refine this picture of the importance of open strings to the cycle.

Friezes 2, 3 and 4 take a rather different form to Frieze 1. They are each built around tiny, recurring motives, which are scattered among the instruments and subject to varying degrees of change. Thus the title refers not to the use of modular form, but rather to the music's somewhat impersonal exploration of permanency and alteration. The 'mobile staticity' that is characteristic of the frieze is reflected in the music's cumulative presentation of altered perspectives on something that is in essence ever-same but whose totality can only be properly appreciated over time. Additionally, Birtwistle suggests that the form of these pieces bears some resemblance to a frieze – though here one must presume that he means the continuous, Ionic frieze rather than the modular Doric one. An Ionic frieze that runs all the way round a room or a building frequently offers no unambiguous starting place; rather it presents a continuous, circular process that one can begin to view at any point. Birtwistle's Friezes, likewise, comprise streams of musical material whose openings and conclusions are largely arbitrary: in Birtwistle's words, they have to be 'faked'.[25]

It would be wrong to give the impression that these three Friezes are identical in their mode of operation. Frieze 2 is the least dependent on recurring motives. Three rather cursory ideas are kept in constant circulation, and underpin a succession of duets between different instruments which carry more continuous material. Frieze 4, which will be discussed in greater detail below, attempts to reconcile motivic recurrence with fugal form. Frieze 3 contains the most extravagant use of motives, some of which are shown in Example 4.4. As in the other two Friezes, these recurring motives are often offset against a more continuous

Example 4.3   Harrison Birtwistle, 'tuning up' music in Fantasia 4

element – an ostinato or a pulse – although these, too, are usually short-lived, constantly reinventing themselves.

Of course, the idea of creating a larger structure by combining a number of recurring smaller elements, each subject to a different degree of change, is far from new in Birtwistle's music. As mentioned above, it is a principle central to the numerous works by Birtwistle that contain an element of verse form. What

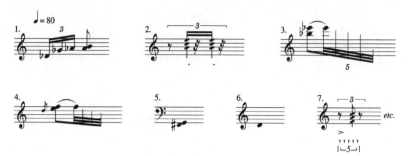

Example 4.4   Harrison Birtwistle, repeated motives in Frieze 3

is new about these quartet movements is the application of the process to such tiny, motivic elements. In *Verses for Ensembles* and *Carmen Arcadiae Mechanicae Perpetuum*, the units subjected to varied repetition comprise larger sections of many bars in length. In Friezes 2, 3 and 4 they are, at most, a handful of notes.

This development, though initially startling to those accustomed to the more homogeneous local progress of Birtwistle's recent music, is in an important sense a logical one. It mirrors on a small scale the way in which Birtwistle's approach to *large scale* structure altered during the 1960s and 1970s. The earliest of Birtwistle's pieces to allude explicitly to verse form tended to content themselves with an interleaving of two types of material – this is the case in works like *The World is Discovered, Three Movements with Fanfares*, and *Verses* for clarinet and piano. In later works, this simple succession of related verses was superseded by more complex and unpredictable multilayered structures. *Verses for Ensembles*, for instance, interleaves seven layers of material, while the later *Carmen Arcadiae Mechanicae Perpetuum* uses six.

The same additional complexity is taken on by Birtwistle's microstructures in the quartet Friezes. This is most clearly seen if the fate of verse structure is followed through into the music of the 1980s and early 1990s. During this period, Birtwistle became increasingly reluctant to transplant musical material from one part of a piece to another, because of the way in which such a strategy seemed to ignore the demands of the immediate musical context. The principle of the 'sanctity of the context' dictated that verse-like repetition was no longer to be found on a large scale in Birtwistle's music. That is not to say that verse structure was abandoned altogether however. Instead, it retreats to the local level, manifesting itself in the varied ostinati and small-scale exchanges from which individual *sections* are still typically built. These local 'verse' structures are particularly audibly apparent in works such as *Earth Dances, Antiphonies* and *The Cry of Anubis*: here, an ostinato pattern may proceed in terms of simple varied repetition, as if it were a succession of altered statements of a single tiny verse; or it may contain a 'call and response' element, and thus sound like *two* contrasting verses interleaved. At any rate, the 'verse structure' of these small-scale ostinati remains simple in these pieces. In the quartet Friezes, on the other hand, the microstructural organization can be seen to have followed the same path of development taken by the large-scale repetitions of Birtwistle's music over 30 years earlier. Now, instead of one or two constituent elements, there are five or seven, intermingled unpredictably. The simple, periodic repetitivity characteristic of the 1980s and early 1990s has given way to a far more complex, though still not unverse-like, patterning.[26]

This development is perhaps most readily appreciated in the last Frieze, which takes its title from Celan's famous poem 'Todesfuge'. I'm going to leave to one side the question of any more explicit connection between Birtwistle's piece and Celan's poem, which draws so directly from the poet's experience of the Holocaust, to focus instead upon the connection that the title establishes with *fugue*. Fugue would seem an incongruous thing to find in Birtwistle. His music certainly often has a contrapuntal character, but it is one that usually arises from the superimposition of *independent* layers of material, rather than from the combination of closely connected parts. The centrality of periodic repetition to fugue, however – that is to say, the fact that, in fugue, the subject constantly reappears – suggests at least a loose connection with one of Birtwistle's principal preoccupations. It is this aspect of fugue that helps make the parallel between Birtwistle's strategy of motivic recurrence in these Friezes, and the complex verse structure of a piece like *Verses for Ensembles*, particularly clear. Birtwistle's 'subject' is not a single, fixed idea, but a collection of five distinct motives (Example 4.5). These motives are initially presented quite separately, one to a bar. The 'answer', in the second violin, repeats the same motives, but in a different order, and in slightly altered versions. The remaining two entries follow exactly the same procedure. Figure 4.3 shows the resulting structure. In this piece the regularity provided by the fugal structure gives an extra layer of formalization to the recurrence of motives, making the correspondence with Birtwistle's earlier treatment of verse forms particularly marked. Much the same sort of unpredictable recurrence is found, on a large scale, in *Verses for Ensembles* and *Carmen Arcadiae Mechanicae Perpetuum*.

Following the initial exposition, Birtwistle's 'fugue' follows a clearly articulated course. This involves the singling out and repetition of individual motives from the subject, sometimes with a close stretto imitation in a second instrument, and then the successive growth in prominence of the two counter-subjects – first the artificial harmonics initially presented in the cello, and then the demisemiquavers that initially appeared in the viola. The latter eventually completely eliminate the subject. Only right at the end of the movement does it return, each of the five motives presented individually in forceful unison (b. 86). Michael Hamburger has described the grim subject matter of Celan's 'Todesfuge' as

Example 4.5   Harrison Birtwistle, five-part subject from Todesfuge – Frieze 4

A B C D E | C D A E B | D A C B E | B D E A C

Figure 4.3   Todesfuge – Frieze 4: resulting structure

'grossly impure' and Arnold Whittall has suggested that Birtwistle, having become intimate with Hamburger's volume of translations, may have conceived of his own fugal material along the same lines.[27] But Hamburger's description may also have coincidentally sewn a connection in Birtwistle's mind with the mightiest precedent for culminating fugue – Beethoven's own 'gross' fugue.[28] The strenuousness of Birtwistle's writing, and the effortful, climactic unison statement of his theme, suggests that the *Grosse Fuge* was never far from his mind. The parallel is instructive. Beethoven's fugue grapples audibly with the awesome responsibility of satisfyingly concluding an unprecedentedly heterogeneous multi-movement work (the B♭ Quartet, Op. 130). It is possible to hear in the fierce ambitiousness of Frieze 4 Birtwistle's own struggle with a similar task. The piece effectively acknowledges the disparateness of the contents of the cycle that it brings so decisively to a close.

Notes

1   Details of first performances are given in Jonathan Cross, *Harrison Birtwistle: Man, Mind, Music* (London: Faber, 2000), pp. 274–5.

2   Michael Hall, *Harrison Birtwistle in Recent Years* (London: Robson Books, 1998), p. 135.

3   *Le marteau sans maître* sets three poems by René Char, and each vocal setting is accompanied by between one and three instrumental commentaries, making three mini-cycles.

4   See my 'A conversation with Harrison Birtwistle', Chapter 7, this volume. Birtwistle wryly observes that the complete cycle was certainly not conceived *tout de suite*, as if 'in some mystic haze'.

5   This performance took place at the Queen Elizabeth Hall at London's South Bank Centre, on 29 April 1996.

6   Hall, *Harrison Birtwistle in Recent Years*, p. 115.

7   For further discussion of Birtwistle's approach to melody, see Robert Adlington, *The Music of Harrison Birtwistle* (Cambridge University Press, 2000), pp. 156–80.

8   Fred Everett Maus, 'Music as drama', *Music Theory Spectrum*, vol. 10 (1988), p. 68.

9   *Ibid.*; my emphasis.

10   *Ibid.*

11   Although *Slow Frieze* was completed in December 1995, a few months before the completion of *Pulse Shadows*, *Slow Frieze* was in fact composed after most of the cycle had been written.

12   Birtwistle, cited in *The Harrison Birtwistle Web-Site*, <http://www.filament. illumin.co.uk/birtwistle/carmen.html>, downloaded 15 July 1997.

13   Elma Sanders, 'Frieze', in Jane Turner, ed., *The Dictionary of Art* (London: Macmillan, 1997), pp. 790–91.

14 Stephen Pruslin, programme note to *Pulse Shadows*.
15 Birtwistle, cited in Ross Lorraine, 'Territorial rites I', *Musical Times* (October 1997), p. 8.
16 Sanders, 'Frieze', pp. 790–91; my emphasis.
17 Andrew Clements, programme note to *Slow Frieze*.
18 Hall, *Harrison Birtwistle in Recent Years*, pp. 76–7.
19 The chronological order of the pieces is: 1. Frieze 1; 2. Fantasia 2; 3. Fantasia 4; 4. Fantasia 5; 5. Frieze 2; 6. Frieze 3; 7. Fantasia 1; 8. Todesfuge – Frieze 4; 9. Fantasia 3.
20 Arnold Whittall, 'The mechanisms of lament: Harrison Birtwistle's *Pulse Shadows*', *Music and Letters*, vol. 80, no. 1 (February 1999), p. 90.
21 Adlington, Chapter 7, this volume.
22 Birtwistle, introductory note to Three Movements for String Quartet (Universal Edition).
23 This motive also makes a fleeting appearance in Fantasia 2 (bb. 6–8) and is alluded to in the coda of Fantasia 1 (bb. 43 ff.).
24 Hall, *Harrison Birtwistle in Recent Years*, p. 77.
25 Adlington, Chapter 7, this volume. In fact, this applies better to Frieze 2 and Frieze 3 than to Frieze 4, which, as a quasi-fugue, inevitably must be seen as predicated upon its opening.
26 The third piece in *Harrison's Clocks* for piano, though written a couple of years after the completion of the Nine Movements, represents a sort of halfway house in this development. Here a number of musical mechanisms recur unpredictably, on each occasion being allowed to run for a few bars before being replaced by a successor. The recurring units are too short to constitute formal sections in the 1960s sense, but too long to be categorized as a single motivic statement (indeed each mechanism is built from a *succession* of repeated motives).
27 Whittall, 'The mechanisms of lament', pp. 96–7.
28 Michael Hall also makes this comparison: *Harrison Birtwistle in Recent Years*, p. 141.

Chapter 5

Precarious Rapture: The Recent Music of Jonathan Harvey

Julian Johnson

> What I seek is music that is as fresh as an improvisation and yet has not a sound out of place.[1]

Jonathan Harvey's remark, made in 1999, highlights a definitive quality of the works he produced during the 1990s. It is a characteristic remark, invoking a paradox fundamental to his music; that through the freedom of individual musical lines a deeper, common order unfolds. If there is a discernible change in Jonathan Harvey's more recent music, it is a matter of emphasis rather than direction. His long-standing concern with underlying principles of order and unity, developed in his study with Erwin Stein, Hans Keller and Milton Babbitt, remain a central part of his compositional technique, but the relationship between these principles and the gestural surface of the music is less consciously ordered and exhibits a greater degree of freedom. It is perhaps the hallmark of a composer's maturity, that the detail comes to embody the principles of the larger whole in such an instinctive way, that the element of construction becomes inaudible.

Neither the mercurial surface play of Harvey's recent music nor the resounding of its global harmonic fields are new, but rather the degree of fluency with which it seems to move between these two dimensions. Indeed, his music is partly defined by this fluency of movement between different musical states – between dance-like metrical clarity and the apparent absence of any temporal division, between foregrounded melodic lines and their dissolution in complex textures, between timbre and harmony. For this reason alone it is hard to generalize about Harvey's music. In the 1990s, for example, works that seem to project a new emphasis on melody sit side by side with works that seem to dissolve away any sense of individual line. More precisely, the two tendencies often coexist in the same work.

A key work in this progress was perhaps *Valley of Aosta* (1988). Harvey's own words, about the work's relation to Turner's painting, highlight its tendency towards the dissolution of individual lines and its emphasis on the moulding of musical energies rather than musical objects:

Turner's *Valley of Aosta: Snowstorm, Avalanche and Thunderstorm (1836)* has no discernible figures or objects; it is an explosion of energy and diffracted light. Like it, my music is constantly shifting and has few firm outlines. Often the harmony is not stated by sustained lines but by short points of sound: it is atomised, pulverised, with light shining through.[2]

In the same programme note, the composer acknowledges a wider influence, pointing to a French cultural tradition evoked in part by the fact that the work was commissioned by the Parisian group L'Itinéraire. He refers to 'a sense of living-in-colour which, at its best, dissolves subject-object duality as idea and colour unite, and thematicism melts into psychic flow'. Harvey's take on this French cultural perspective may be idiosyncratic but it points to an important *musical* influence that has become increasingly significant for him. One might recall Boulez in reading Harvey's description of the musical sound as 'atomised' and 'pulverised', or his account of the last of the three computer-driven sequences for synthesizers in which 'the rapid succession of pitches whirls fragments from earlier in the piece along in a kind of spray, eventually dissolving all distinct shape'. It would be hard to mistake two such individual musical voices, but in a work like *Valley of Aosta* one can hear a shared fascination with the visceral energy of coruscating textures, and the liminal thrill produced by 'objectless' musical sonorities.

But if there is a relation to Boulez it is not so much one of influence as having both been subject to similar forces. Despite the difference in age, temperament and cultural background, there is a parallel between Harvey and Boulez in the way that a concern with the strict ordering principles of post-Webernian serialism has been subsequently overlaid with no less a fascination for the music of Debussy. The 'uniting of idea and colour' exemplified in Debussy's music might seem opposed to the tradition of Austro-German thematicism whose essentially abstract premise is made explicit in serialism. Harvey's development of electronic music at Institut de Recherche et Coordination Acoustique/Musique (IRCAM) was, not coincidentally, allied with the emergence of a more obviously French element in his work. In Debussy the musical idea is not separable from its specific manifestation – an approach to music rooted in the acoustic characteristics of its sonorous materials exemplified in the predominantly French exploration of spectralism.

But while sound itself has long been a central concern of Harvey's music, it is perhaps in his attitude to form that Debussy's influence becomes most important in the 1990s. It is not that earlier global structuring devices are abandoned – such as symmetrical harmonic fields – but that, in certain works, the music takes on a greater freedom, a new-found confidence to elaborate less rhetorical and more improvisatory structures. It seems, at times, as if music here has become more resistant to being grasped as a solid object. The Percussion Concerto (1997) provides a good example. There is a cultivated quality of insubstantiality about much of this work, not just in its often understated use of the orchestra, but in the deliberately fragmentary presentation of its materials. Indeed, what exactly constitutes the musical material remains elusive, as the fleeting snippets of solo and ensemble statements resist being grasped by the mind. It is music that cultivates the thresholds of perception, appearing and disappearing, offering some just-graspable formal shape and then dissolving it again in order to reform it in the next moment (qualities shared with other works of the same period such as *Ashes Dance Back* and *Wheel of Emptiness*, both also from 1997).

The Percussion Concerto tends to avoid the overtly dramatic dialogue one might traditionally expect from the concerto genre, and which is still vestigially present at points of the earlier Cello Concerto (1990). It plays less with dialogue and more with the infinite prismatic refractions of a single voice, whose identity is constantly dissolved as material is passed quickly around the orchestra. This ephemeral, constantly shifting quality is shared equally by the slow central movement, which likewise treads a fine line between the barely perceptible and the just imperceptible, creating a sound world that is as ungraspable as the 'atmosphere' that it generates. Even in the third and faster movement, characterized by a greater metrical regularity and rhythmic energy, the same lightness of touch helps avoid any statement that is too substantial or heavy, any gesture that is too obvious. (Example 5.1).

While the role of the soloist in the Cello Concerto is more clearly differentiated from the orchestra, the same improvisatory qualities are found here too. The solo part is frequently marked 'free' (a characteristic Harvey instruction) but also often with a qualifier: 'Free: precariously rapturous' or 'Free: intensely enrapt'. But it is not just the material itself that seems free, but its sequential patterning through the piece as a whole. The solo part is sometimes marked 'as if continuing', implying that tutti passages relate to solo passages more like parentheses than part of a linear discourse. For all that there *is* a larger shape to this deliberately loose, associative patterning: the piece seems to work *towards* a melodic statement, as if melody were the goal of the piece, a formal shape repeated in a number of Harvey's works of this period.

The String Quartet No. 3 (1995) provides a good example of this melody-orientated form. Harvey's concern for the fleeting and ephemeral qualities of sound here reaches a new height: the treatment of the quartet creates textures which resist the ear settling on any particular figure or instrument. At its premiere, and in a number of subsequent performances, it has been programmed alongside Webern's *Six Bagatelles for String Quartet*, Op. 9, a work whose ungraspable soundworld seems to provide the starting point for Harvey's. But amid the web of otherworldly sounds, achieved through an almost complete avoidance of 'naturale' scoring, Harvey allows fragmentary melodic gestures to emerge – brief moments of rapturous lyricism amid the otherwise elusive composite textures of the ensemble. There is a clear sense of progression in the way in which these melodic gestures begin to coalesce, and the work ends with a particularly striking example of one of Harvey's sustained melodies, here in the upper reaches of the violin's register, marked variously 'sweet', 'serene', and 'tender' (Example 5.2).

Example 5.1   Jonathan Harvey, Percussion Concerto, 1st movement, J to M

Example 5.1   continued

Example 5.1   continued

Example 5.1   continued

Aspects of British Music of the 1990s

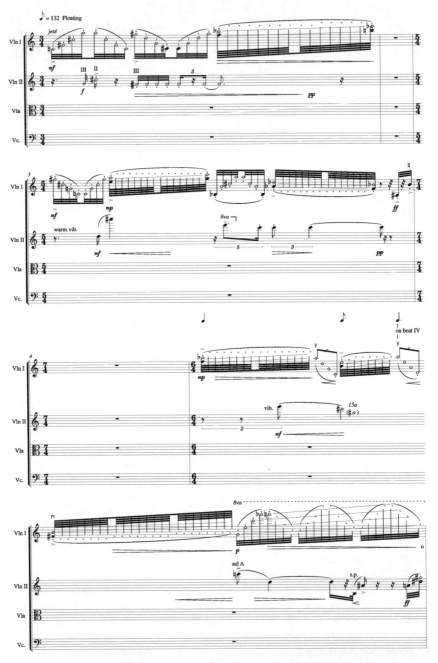

**Example 5.2   Jonathan Harvey, String Quartet no. 3, opening, pp. 1–2
(bars 1–5)**

In some works, the narrative trajectory of this 'moving towards melody' is made explicit. In *Scena* (1992) for example, the five sections of the work are given titles, underlining their sequence as dramatic events in this 'quasi-operatic scene.' The titles themselves (Lament, Mystical Event, Romantic Event, Dream, Metamorphosis) recall Webern again, through their similarity to the titles he once gave the movements of his *Five Pieces for Orchestra*, Op. 10 (Original Form, Metamorphosis, Return, Remembrance, Soul). More specifically, they relate quite directly to the concerns of the actual operatic project which Harvey had just completed, *Inquest of Love*, a work whose particular version of 'darkness to light' clearly lies behind the structure of *Scena*. In both works, the transfigurative 'mystical event' makes possible the rapturous lyricism of the music that follows it – here, once again, in the peculiarly intense upper register of the violin.

The timbral aspect of Harvey's melodic rapture is significant: it recalls the human voice at the same time as it leaves it behind. Both the violin and the cello (favourite choices for the lyrical moment) sing in their upper registers with an intensity quite unlike any other instrument. It comes closest to that of the human voice while clearly being 'superhuman' on account of its register. Such moments in Harvey's music invoke a long tradition in western music by which the upper register of a solo violin is explicitly associated not only with a feminine voice but with a specifically angelic one.

These concerns are central to a work the Cello Concerto anticipates and which *Scena* follows – the two-act opera, *Inquest of Love* (1992). The link is made explicit, in that melodic material from the opera (sung by Ann, the main female protagonist) is also given to the solo cello in the concerto. The opera was com-missioned by English National Opera and premiered at the Coliseum in 1993. While not Harvey's first opera (*Passion and Resurrection* dates from 1981), it was nevertheless his first work for a traditional opera house. His response to the peculiar challenge of writing a work in the context of such a weighty historical tradition as grand opera is revealing. To hear that the opera is set largely in a monastery and begins and ends with the sound of its abbot's quiet breathing during meditation might suggest that the composer's interest in the timeless is here at odds with the operatic expectations of narrative drama. But these expec-tations are in fact the central material of the opera which is predicated on revealing the wider context in which a one-dimensional temporal unfolding of the narrative takes place.

Its concern is the necessity of time for the revelation of the timeless: in T.S. Eliot's words: 'only through time time is conquered'.[3] The action as such is rela-tively simple: John and Ann are to be married by the Abbot, but the wedding service is interrupted by the arrival of Ann's sister Elspeth who, in revenge for some past mistreatment, shoots Ann dead. This event is re-enacted two more times within the first act; at its third occurrence Elspeth shoots John before turning the gun on herself. This overturning of a naturalistic narrative leads the opera's story away from the concrete and literal realm in which it began. Between

the second and third occurrence of the shooting incident three 'heavenly' characters make their appearance – guides for the inward journey that the three human
characters have now to make. Only when Ann and John are able to forgive
Elspeth, through understanding her suffering, is the frozen situation in which they
are all held able to move forward: with the release that comes with this forgiveness, new life is made possible. The opera ends with a fourth (and this time
successful) enactment of the wedding ceremony.

Such a scenario, concerned with problematizing the very nature of naturalistic linear time and exploring instead a sense of inward rather than outward
unfolding of events, presents a composer with some very specific problems. For
Harvey, however, these problems lie at the heart of his compositional quest – to
create a musical form that unfolds through linear time while being contained
within a global or vertical time. *Inquest of Love* presents a fragment of literal
narrative (the wedding ceremony) but its treatment of this fragment, through
repetition and a kind of analysis not confined to the chronological, opens up
other temporal strategies: of inward journeys which also have their events and
intensities while, outwardly, time is suspended. The return to the wedding ceremony at the end of the opera implies that 'no time has passed' since the same
ceremony began in the first act; the immense journeys of self-exploration,
understanding, suffering and forgiveness have, as it were, happened out of ordinary narrative time, yet are made available to us only through their narration on
stage.

This comes close to the core of Harvey's work, but it is by no means one
confined to the subtleties of the texts he sets or of his own extra-musical reflections on composition. It is, rather, something rooted in the compositional techniques which characterize his musical language. Perhaps, for some, to speak of
angels takes us too close to the personal symbols and images of the composer
himself, a reproduction of a composer's idiosyncratic field of reference that critical commentary should avoid. But it is hard to avoid such terms discussing
Harvey's music, if only because they mark cultural ideas which the music itself
embodies. I do not mean that Harvey's music literally evokes images or ideas of
the angelic (although it is possible that it might for some listeners); I mean rather
that the idea of the angelic acts as a symbol for the idea of transcendence, a term
which has a direct and precise value in discussing aspects of the music.

Perhaps the music of Jonathan Harvey is hardly comprehensible without
recourse to such terms. To place his music in relation to other music at the end of
the twentieth century requires more than a catalogue of works and compositional
techniques. One can label him in various ways – as a modernist, as an electro-
acoustic composer, as a spectralist – or one can list salient techniques – symmetrical harmonic fields, melodic transformations, timbral modulation. But compositional techniques are not atomistic, interchangeable ingredients of a composer's
style; they are the tools of a composer's idea, refined over a lifetime to embody
that idea more precisely. If Jonathan Harvey's music is often discussed in terms

that border on the metaphysical, this is more than a reporting of the composer's own field of reference. It points to the fact that his music inherits the central metaphysical assumptions of early modernism: that art shapes its materials in order to point beyond them and to project an order over and against the materials which it shapes. In this way, all music worth the name is transcendent – or, in Harvey's own words: 'In a metaphysical sense music never changes: it always portrays the play of the Relative against the ground of the Absolute.'[4]

This is not hard to demonstrate. Consider, for example, *Advaya* (1994) for solo cello and electronics. The title means literally 'not-two' – about as succinct a statement of Harvey's aesthetic as one could hope to find. It is not called 'One' because Harvey's music is a long way from a kind of new-age ambience. It is concerned rather with the *point* or *moment* of transcendence, the borderlands in which individual elements (a single note, a motif) partake of two intersecting identities (a linear, intervallic one, and a vertical, timbral-harmonic one). The music dwells on the ambiguity of these two identities – the fact that the same element coexists in the two dimensions simultaneously. In dialogue with the electronics the solo cello quite literally transcends itself through the use of virtuosic extended techniques (or 'transcendental technique' as Liszt might have said). But as the electronics literally 'go beyond' the cello's sound – into realms which a 'live' cello could not go – it does so not by doing something wholly different but by a transformation of the cello's own sound. Indeed, the entire piece is derived from a spectral analysis of the cello's open A string, its essential 'nature' if you like. But while the acoustic cello pushes the limits of what it can produce from that A string, the electronic transformations project sounds derived entirely from the same source, but beyond the reach of the 'live' performer (Example 5.3).

Transcendence here is not some 'extra' interpretative gloss of the composer – it is as precise as any other analytical category in denoting the structural relationship in *Advaya* between the acoustic cello and the electronics. In its temporal unfolding the piece quite literally enacts transcendence. At times the cello celebrates its own materiality as a sound-producing object – at one point the body of the instrument (whose resemblance to the human body has often been noted) is used as a drum. In concert with the electronics it produces a tabla-like sound which forms the basis of a more corporeal dance section. But at other times a combination of extended techniques and electronic transformations produces a radically desubstantialized sound which has no immediate relation to any concrete sound-producing object (such as the rapid sweeping gestures towards the end of the piece which recall Harvey's discussion of the ending to *Valley of Aosta*).

For Harvey himself, of course, this technical capacity for transcendence has a more than musical or sonic aspect. In his recent book, *In Quest of Spirit*, he suggested that whereas electronic music was the single most important *technical* breakthrough in music of the twentieth century, spectralism was a breakthrough

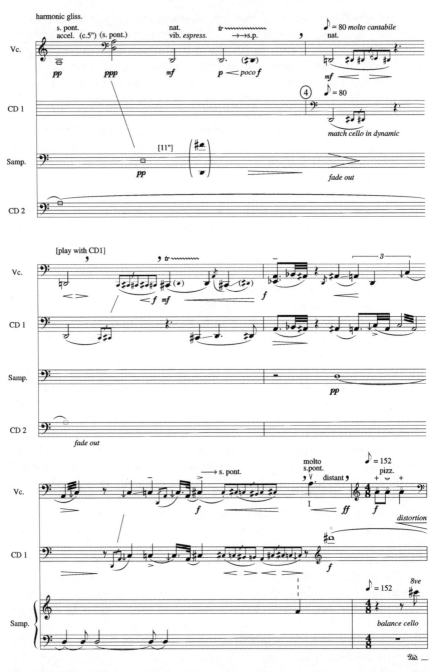

Example 5.3　Jonathan Harvey, *Advaya*, pp. 8–9

Example 5.3   continued

of *spiritual* significance. While he admits that this may be a partial view, it points nevertheless to the capacity of spectralism to deal more directly with the physical nature of musical sound, and thus of our understanding of time and space, than was hitherto possible. It has clearly been a dominant concern of his in the 1990s, and he touches on it several times in recent writings. With hindsight he refers back to a number of 'proto-spectralists' (including not only Messiaen but also the composer of *Parsifal!*) but in his own work at least it was the tape piece *Mortuos plango, vivos voco*, produced at IRCAM in 1980, that first brought this approach to the foreground. This way of thinking about sound, based on the computer analysis of the harmonic spectra of single sounds, was developed principally at IRCAM and associated with figures such as Gérard Grisey and Tristan Murail. It is perhaps Jonathan Harvey's exposure to this way of thinking – and enthusiasm for it – that distinguishes him most obviously from other English composers of his generation. It has shaped not only his music for tape and live electronics, but also the way in which he has come to write for acoustic instruments – as is amply demonstrated both by works which include electronics, such as *Advaya*, and those which do not, such as the String Quartet, no.3.

The individuality of Harvey's approach to spectralism lies perhaps in his interest in exploring the interface not just between acoustic and electronic sound, but between the global dimension of harmonic spectra and their specific exploration in the unfolding of individual pieces. There is a potential for stasis in the contemplation of spectra which certainly informs Harvey's music, but it is more often placed alongside music of great energy and dynamism. And it is precisely this interpenetration of two dimensions, of the vertical and the horizontal, the global and the linear, which seems to fascinate him as a composer. For him, the vertical proportions of a sound, as laid out in its harmonic spectrum, may also be unfolded horizontally.

> The fascination of spectral thinking is that it, too, can easily shift into the realm of linear time, into melodic thinking: there is a large borderland of ambiguity to exploit ... Intervallicism can shade into and out of spectralism, and it is in this ambiguity that much of the richness in the approach lies.[5]

It is for this reason that a confirmed spectralist such as Harvey can also write an opera. What distinguishes Harvey's music is that it brings the insights of abstract computer research into play with formal concerns that retain their links to some age-old narrative paradigms. Chief among these is that of a journey – from dark to light, low to high, formlessness to form, stasis to energy, and so on. At the same time, what distinguishes these patterns in his music from, say, their treatment in Classical and Romantic music, is that one term of the duality does not obliterate the other. Instead, the music's journey is shaped around a revelation of their unbreakable relationship; it alters the balance of its dualistic poles while preserving both as aspects of the same thing.

Example 5.4   Jonathan Harvey, *Soleil Noir/Chitra*, pp. 45–8, BB to DD (12 bars)

Much of Harvey's music might be read in terms of its musical journey from dark to light and this remains a central metaphor of more recent works such as *Scena, Inquest of Love* or *Ashes Dance Back* (1997). In some cases, the duality is marked even in the title, as in *Soleil Noir/Chitra* (1995) or *Death of Light/Light of Death* (1998). No matter which descriptive metaphor one employs, the unfolding of a musical journey seems self-evident. These works have their own rates of movement, stases, apparent loss of direction, doubt, renewed energy, clarity, dramatic events, moments of arrival and, at times, of epiphany. As the works with

Example 5.4   continued

text make explicit, for Harvey this journey is also a transfigurative or even redemptive process, a concern underlined in his oratorio for the BBC Proms in 2000, *Mothers Shall not Cry*. But Harvey's music is not lacking in elements of the 'negativity' so often associated with musical modernism. It often requires these as the necessary beginning of its musical journey, such as the agitated passages of palpable violence for double bass, cello, trombone and tuba of the *Soleil Noir* which alternate with the brighter energy of *Chitra* (Example 5.4). But the larger structural process of these works is to reveal the darker elements as part of a larger harmonic whole, conceived vertically as a spectral relationship. And in this

Example 5.4   continued

'revelation' (the gift of the unfolding musical process) the violent energy of lower partials finds repose when heard as part of the greater harmony of the complete spectrum.

In Harvey's own words, his recent music is shaped by 'an aesthetic of spectral hide-and-seek' in which material presented linearly, as melody, is then revealed as contained within a vertically disposed harmonic spectrum.[6] This sense of 'being between two worlds' is perhaps the essence of his musical style, both technically and aesthetically. There is much about Harvey's music that suggests an ultra-modern complex world of computer technology and advanced

Example 5.4   continued

compositional technique and, on one level, his music is certainly little
concerned with the everyday or prosaic. But, by the same token, his music
derives from archaic roots – from a concern with the mythic, magical properties
of musical sound and its potential to mediate our sense of self and other, of
individual and whole. In his most recent music, this orientation towards the
timeless as the defining characteristic of the radically new has become explicit
in a particularly simple way.

Example 5.5   Jonathan Harvey, *Calling Across Time*, pp. 3–5, B to D (13 bars)

Arnold Whittall, discussing the recent orchestral work *Calling Across Time* (1998), drew attention to the 'rootedness' of its harmonic world and Harvey's new-found appetite for 'relatively stable consonance'.[7] It is a work which exemplifies a confidence to employ materials which, for many modernist composers, have long been proscribed. The wind instruments are here frequently deployed in antiphonal, chorale-like homophony, characterized by harmony which recalls the spacing and motion of a triadic system (Example 5.5). But this gesture is no mere

Example 5.5   continued

archaicism: it is one possible permutation of the harmonic substance which
Harvey's music deploys. So too, the rare but arresting moments of triadic consonance in *Advaya* or *White as Jasmine* (1999) bear little relation to the unprepared
and superficial consonances which sometimes appeared at the end of otherwise
atonal avant-garde pieces by certain composers in the 1970s. The harmonic world
of Jonathan Harvey's more recent works is, strictly speaking, not atonal. Perhaps
one could begin to speak here of a 'spectral tonality', a harmony based on inclusiveness and balance of its elements rather than hierarchical opposition, a harmony
in which the individual line freely elaborates its own identity through time but
which is, at the same time, completed by the revelation of its place within a

Example 5.5 continued

greater timeless order. Caught between the tugging of these two orders, it is here perhaps that Jonathan Harvey's music finds its unique quality of 'precarious rapture'.

Notes

1 Interview comment printed in Arnold Whittall, *Jonathan Harvey* (London: Faber, 1999), p. 32.
2 Programme note by the composer, printed in the score to *Valley of Aosta* (London: Faber Music, 1993).

3   T.S. Eliot, 'Burnt Norton' from 'Four Quartets' in *The Complete Poems and Plays of T.S. Eliot* (London: Faber and Faber, 1969), p. 173.

4   Jonathan Harvey, 'Reflection after composition', *Contemporary Music Review*, vol. 1, no. 1 (1984), p. 86.

5   Jonathan Harvey, *In Quest of Spirit* (Berkeley, CA: University of California Press, 1999), p. 40.

6   J. Harvey, *In Quest of Spirit* (Berkeley: University of California Press, 1999), p. 41.

7   Whittall, *Jonathan Harvey*, pp. 80–81.

Chapter 6

Perception of Structure: *Sonata-Rondo* for Piano (1996)

Sebastian Forbes

Whether talking or writing, I have constantly warned about the danger of the task I am here invited to enter upon – that of attempting to explain my own music, with a view to helping others to understand it more fully. Of course there is much that any composer can say about his own work, but, as Peter Evans once summarized,[1] I speak as one who 'distrusts analytical explanations as likely to come between the music and the listener's experience'. So, although encouraged to be closely analytical,[2] I decided to widen the scope and include some consideration of what the astute listener might be able to *perceive* in a work's structure, rather than focus merely upon the technical armoury by which it is achieved.

Such technical armoury is, of course, a means to an end. But this 'end', the 'message' of a piece, is less easily defined. It may even be multi-layered, as for instance in a work such as Beethoven's *Missa Solemnis*: here is a world-embracing work if ever there was one, and yet its score is headed with an aphorism that suggests an intimate, personal communication: 'Von Herzen – möge es wieder zu Herzen gehen' ('From my heart – may it arrive at the heart of others'). Instrumental, abstract music, devoid of text or evident non-musical associations, poses a special challenge. Whatever the piece of music, however, if listening is to be deeper than merely hearing, if true attention demands a measure of listening that one might call intellectual, as an extension of the intuitive,[3] then we should recognize the presence of understanding. But what is 'understanding? Consider the following:

> You don't need to know about music to enjoy it. And it is tempting to conclude from this that you don't need to know about music to understand it, either. After all, if you have enjoyment, who needs understanding? In which case, what possible reason can there be for adding the -ology to music?[4]

> For there are two ways in which men's minds want to 'understand' works of art: the first and primal, by the path of sensitive aesthetic apprehension; the second and cerebral, by the path of analysis. This latter has many side-tracks leading nowhere, and the only way of avoiding them is to make sure, through the test of audibility, that the path of analysis and the path of aesthetic apprehension are going the same way.[5]

There is no substitute for listening – whatever instances may be afforded by the debat-able methods of musical 'analysis'. As the philosopher demonstrated the reality of motion by walking, so the reality of musical form is grasped by listening. Performance is the 'moment of truth' ... A work of art is not something to be explained. Only growing familiarity with it will lead to true participation – which I prefer to the word 'understanding'[6]

All analysis which precedes musical understanding – that is, the intuitive artistic experience – replaces the work of art instead of reflecting it ... The artistic mind analyses, or needs analysis, because it understands, not because it doesn't.[7]

Notice that all four writers refer to understanding, each with a slightly different slant, and sometimes suggesting a need for qualification. If all four were to be brought together and asked to define 'understanding', the debate would be heated, more so perhaps on the definition of terms than on the matter itself. I cite the above in order to illustrate the difficulty, but I now turn to the matter itself, with my own work as a case study.

We should begin by agreeing that artistic experience begins with listening, not explaining. Such explaining can only, at best, follow the experience, hopefully to enrich it rather than reduce it. So, how should a composer introduce his work, to an audience who is about to hear it? What should a programme note contain? Here, I try to consider what an eager listener would be glad to know, before hearing the work, though, as composers have often shown, it is tempting to say too much. I once illustrated this point by reference to the visual arts, indicating that, before you become fully engaged in the appreciation of a painting, a sculp-ture, or a building, you can grasp its size, its basic material (for example oil on canvas, wood-cut, marble sculpture, stone or brick, and so on) and something about subject-matter and/or purpose.[8] But you cannot see music (the score is a mere representation of the music, not the music itself). So what are the equival-ents in aural terms?

Two factors are obvious: the basic material, in the case of my *Sonata-Rondo*, is the piano, and its 'size' is its duration. The first would be covered by the title of the piece and the nature of the event, but the second should, I feel, be mentioned in a note. After all, you pace your mode of reception differently when you listen to a concentrated piece by Webern from when you hear an extended piece by Steve Reich.

But what of subject matter and purpose? About as far as one should go, I would suggest, is contained in my note for the premiere:

This one-movement work, lasting just under 15 minutes, is dedicated to Jana Frenklova and is now receiving its first performance. Its general seriousness of purpose and careful design suggested the 'Sonata' part of the title (akin to my many ensemble sonatas), while the pattern of thematic returns suggested 'Rondo' (akin to many works in what could be described as 'mosaic' form).

Sonata-Rondo has eight 'themes', which return in different ways, making 25 sections in all. The most obvious aspect of this is how the opening introspective chordal passage gradually gives way to the spacious second theme (which closes the work), or, put in more dramatic terms, frustration gradually finding release in open space.[9]

That is sufficient for the initial 'enjoyment', 'sensitive aesthetic apprehension', 'moment of truth', or 'intuitive artistic experience'. Comparing this stage with deeper acquaintance prompts us to define two stages of familiarization, which we might find useful:

(a) awareness of the presence and effect of structure
(b) ability to identify its elements and operation.

My programme note attempts no more than would encourage stage (a) and avoids more than a mere hint of (b), in which only the keenest listener would be able or motivated to indulge on first hearing. In elaborating a little further, I could eluci- date by describing the two main 'themes' (each occurring five times) as repre- senting a 'cross-fade': the first theme is commanding at the opening and the second theme follows as a mere subsidiary; in the course of the work, the first theme's reappearances become progressively shorter, while the second grows in importance until it dominates the final pages. Other themes are arranged in between these, and the reappearances of all themes lend a measure of structural balance and intelligibility which supports my aims in creating a traditionalist balance between the architectural (static) and the dramatic (narrative), plus the psychological reassurance of back-references, the sense of direction provided by goals, the interest gained from varied repeats, and so on. Add to this the less predictable effect of mosaic design, which places each return of a theme in a different context – an aspect of such working which I have for years found fasci- nating.

But wait: I am already tempting fate, as I am aware that readers may not have heard the work or have a ready opportunity of doing so.[10] Interest in what follows may be restricted to those who have been able to hear the work or possibly those who are curious to know about some of my methods of composing, at least as revealed in this piece. Those who have not heard it should endeavour to imagine an impression of it, as described above, and to keep (a), above, in mind, so that discussion of (b) makes some sense. Otherwise the ensuing discussion may appear to be a series of 'side-tracks leading nowhere', lacking 'the test of audi- bility' (see Graham George, above).

I now wish to take four aspects of the work in turn.

1   *The 'cross-fade' idea*. If a given idea, in a succession of appearances, is to grow or diminish audibly, then it must be instantly recognizable. This can be done by giving it a clear identity (texture, rhythm, and so on) and making it largely non-developmental so that its sound-world remains relatively

**Example 6.1(a)   Sebastian Forbes, *Sonata-Rondo* for Piano (1996),
                     Theme a, start of first occurrence (section 1)**

**Example 6.1(b)   Sebastian Forbes, *Sonata-Rondo* for Piano (1996),
                     Theme a, final occurrence (section 24)**

constant. The first theme, which, as the programme note suggested, we might
call the 'frustration' motif, is characterized by quick staccato chords in close
formation, with groups of chords separated by brief, half-value rests. Example
6.1 shows (a) the opening – about half of section 1 – and (b) theme a's final,
briefest appearance in the penultimate section.

Standing in contrast to this is theme b, the 'open space' motif, which is tiny in section 2 but expands fully at the close – see Example 6.2, (a) and (b).

With their respective identities clearly established, the cross-fade process can be followed. This, to me, lends a sense of goal-directedness to the work as a whole, and provides a framework in which the other themes can take their place and 'play their part'.

2 *Other forms of variation.* Here are three themes each of which occurs just twice. In theme c, the later occurrence is identical in rhythm and duration but enriched in harmony and texture to achieve the opposite in dynamics and mood. Example 6.3 shows the opening seven bars of each (a) and (b).

Next, Example 6.4(a) shows a theme of stillness, theme d complete, while Example 6.4(b) shows the same material returning, in a more agitated manner. Both passages feature a descent from the first chord to the last but are otherwise objective in manner; this is achieved by internal symmetry: the retrograde inversion is identical.

Example 6.5(a) shows a reflective moment – the start of theme e – where harmony colours the note F#, while Example 6.5(b) shows the start of this theme's varied return later in the piece.

3 *Symmetry.* Already touched upon above, this has been a particular preoccupation of mine for decades, even before I consciously felt any influence of Webern or Messiaen in the early 1960s, and perhaps reaches its fullest expression in this work. At a local level we may cite section 16, the third (and shortest) version of theme g, which is here used cadentially – see Example 6.6.

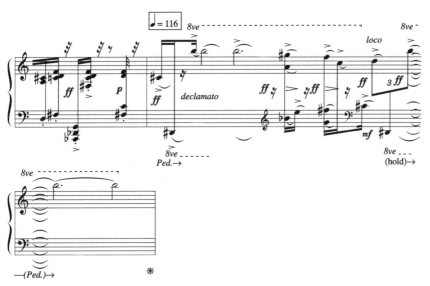

Example 6.2(a) **Sebastian Forbes, *Sonata-Rondo* for Piano (1996),**
Theme b, first occurrence (section 2)

Example 6.2(b)   **Sebastian Forbes, *Sonata-Rondo* for Piano (1996),**
Theme b, final occurrence (section 25)

Example 6.2(b)   continued

The first phrase is immediately answered by its transposed retrograde; thereafter everything is vertically symmetrical, in that the whole passage would be identical if inverted.

Further examples of this can be found in themes a and b (see Example 6.1 and Example 6.2, above) and in other themes which we will discuss later.

At a larger level, in addition to theme d already cited, we may note the three occurrences (sections 7, 13, and 19) of theme f, which are, as it were, inside-out versions of each other. Example 6.7 shows the first occurrence (section 7) complete. The astute reader will sense the symmetry imparted by the

**Example 6.3(a)   Sebastian Forbes, *Sonata-Rondo* for Piano (1996),
Theme c, start of first occurrence (section 4)**

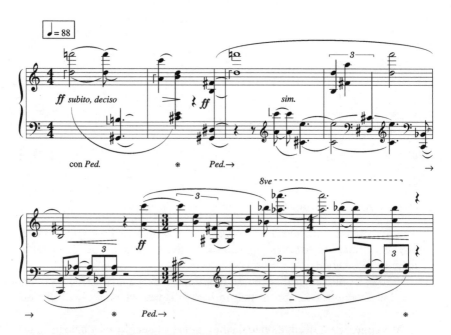

**Example 6.3(b)   Sebastian Forbes, *Sonata-Rondo* for Piano (1996),
Theme c, start of later occurrence (section 22)**

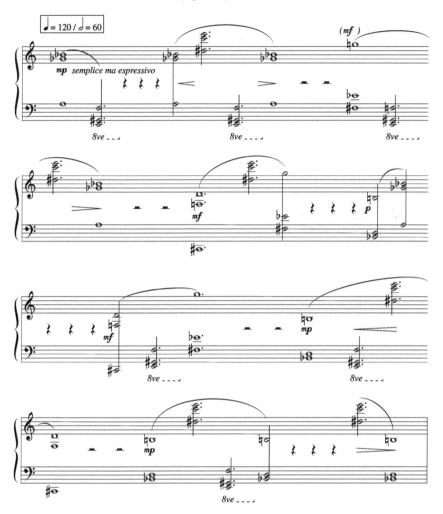

Example 6.4(a)   Sebastian Forbes, *Sonata-Rondo* for Piano (1996),
Theme d, first occurrence (section 5)

palindromic shape of this passage, the D natural immediately after the dimin-
uendo to p commencing a retrograde inversion of the preceding material.

Section 19, the third occurrence of this theme, inverts the opening *mister-
ioso* flourish (V–W) and then proceeds with an exact inversion of W–Z (or
retrograde of Z–W, which is the same thing). In between, centrally to the
whole work, section 13 begins with Y–Z (or the retrograde inversion of X–
W), followed by V–W inverted, then V–W prime, and concluding with W–X
or the retrograde inversion of Z–Y. Let me hasten to add that such processes

Example 6.4(b)   Sebastian Forbes, *Sonata-Rondo* for Piano (1996), Theme d, later occurrence (section 17)

Example 6.5(a)   Sebastian Forbes, *Sonata-Rondo* for Piano (1996),
Theme e, start of first occurrence (section 9)

of composing gave me just what I wanted at these points in the work; otherwise I would not have proceeded in this way. The results, to me, captured the
intended mood of introspection, which is further coloured by the two concur-
rent types of rhythm: metrical, dotted (legato), and more free, with constant
local accelerando or ritardando (staccato).

Symmetry is also found at a structural level, to be illustrated more fully
below.

4   *Progressive tonality.* This is a useful term to denote a regular succession of
pitch-reference centres. 'Tonality' is to be considered here in a flexible sense:
referential pitch class is more accurate, though cumbersome – so, we will abbre-
viate it as 'rpc'. Again, I have been drawn to this sort of procedure for decades,
and in the case of this work it is a factor that may be felt in performance though
not necessarily recognized for what it is. Simply put, the rpc for each section
drops by one semitone. It can readily be realized that, over 25 sections, the final
one is built around the same pitch as the first, D, and that this same reference
informs section 13 (which appropriately avoids either theme a or theme b).

Figure 6.1 (see page 100) shows the overall plan in straightforward, diagrammatic
form.

Naturally Figure 6.1 shows, as simply as possible, what happens in what order,
without revealing the detail of relative durations, and in this respect is no more
accurate proportionally than the standard map of the London Underground.[11] In
addition to the varying durations of themes a and b, I need also to point out that

Example 6.5(b)   Sebastian Forbes, *Sonata-Rondo* for Piano (1996),
Theme e, start of later occurrence (section 21)

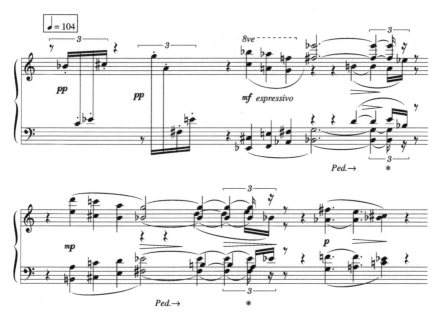

Example 6.6 **Sebastian Forbes, *Sonata-Rondo* for Piano (1996),**
Theme g, third occurrence (section 16)

an exact symmetry of durations would detract from the feeling of onward
momentum. It would not be dramatically appropriate, for instance, if the central
section was exactly central. In fact some of the later recurrences tend to be
slightly shorter, and the final appearance of theme h, section 18, is much longer
and the most climactic of the three: see Example 6.8. This is one way of helping
an architectural plan to support the momentum of narrative.

Figure 6.1 also clarifies which themes relate to which pitch references. Theme
f is symmetrically arranged, built on Ab–D–Ab, notes that feature in all three
occurrences. Themes d and e complement each other by respectively referring to
Bb and F#, equally distant from the main centre of D, and the complementary
nature of the pitching of themes g and h is similarly satisfying. Theme **c** appears
twice, as the fourth section in from each end, first built around B and later around
F, again centres that are equally distant from D.

That leaves themes a and b, and it can now be seen that, in addition to their
variability in duration, contrast is enhanced by their recurrences always coming at
a different pitch.

In all the above, I have talked about sections being built around a pitch class
rather than being in a key in the conventional sense. As in much of my music
that relies on pitch-class referencing, whether in the manner of a passacaglia

**Example 6.7   Sebastian Forbes, *Sonata-Rondo* for Piano (1996),
                 Theme f, first occurrence (section 7)**

(*Sinfonia 1* for orchestra, or String Quartet No. 1: last movement) or in pursuit
of 'progressive tonality' as here (or other works such as *Partita* for clarinet, cello
and piano, or *Hymn to St Etheldreda*), the rpc is rarely a key in the traditional
sense.[12] Rather it is a central note on which the harmonic structure relies in some

Example 6.7   continued

prominent way. Often it is a matter of vertical symmetry, and a further glance at the extracts from themes a and b (see Examples 6.1 and 6.2) will make this clear: in theme a, all the chords are equally above or below the rpc; in theme b, the rpc is essentially in the middle of the harmonic complex, which then tends to explore higher notes a little more than lower ones, for the sake of the desired sonority. Other themes can be related, some easily, some with greater difficulty, to the relevant rpcs, but it should be stressed that this sort of technical detail is not one that any listener could be expected to spot, even in the course of hearing the work several times. Indeed, some listeners may feel tempted to dismiss much of the above discussion as mere games with numbers and devices. Others may not perceive any of this, preferring to regard the work as a free improvisation. Actually there is some validity in both responses. However, my firm view is that, if such means help the composer to achieve his desired task, then fine, and this work would, to me, lack coherence and structure if such technical support and operational precision were not present.

I am sure that the majority of composers would agree with such a view in principle (though not specifically), namely that a vast array of technical armoury lies just beneath the surface of much of their music. Of this array, some facets can eventually be spotted, many not, but all are important in that they add to the strength and conviction of the whole enterprise. This brings us right back to the title of this chapter, and to my view that the intelligent listener, who is prepared for 'sensitive aesthetic apprehension' or 'intuitive artistic experience', will be able to perceive the presence of a structure and a few obvious aspects of it – in this case the framework of the 'cross-fade', the interlocking of various sections and

Section	Rpc	Theme	Correspondences

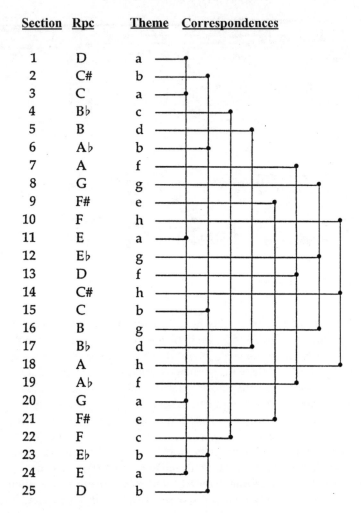

Figure 6.1   Overall plan

their varied returns. All this will add up to the impression of an exciting drama, perhaps analogous to the interaction of different characters on the stage. Much else that I have revealed may only be of peripheral interest.

Further, I have not dwelt extensively on a question that is often raised at seminars given by composers on their work – 'How do you get your notes?' – and nor would this be the place to indulge in such personal matters, over and above some of the obvious pointers that I have indicated. Indeed, such a question is often impossible to answer fully, except to admit that each composer

Example 6.8 Sebastian Forbes, *Sonata-Rondo* for Piano (1996),
Theme h, third occurrence (section 18)

Example 6.8   continued

has a range of favoured harmonic, melodic and rhythmic constructs that tend to dominate his compositional thinking. That is one aspect of what one could call 'style'.

As for the more structuralist approach, touched upon above, and in defence of some of my more arcane procedures, the fact remains that for centuries composers have been fascinated by this sort of mental exercise, and it would be easy to cite many composers of this inclination working in the UK today. What is sometimes not so widely recognized is the extent to which composers of the past indulged in patterns and calculations. Some, like Debussy and Bartók, with their fascination with the Golden Section and its numerical equivalents (best expressed in terms of the Fibonacci series) were, so far as one can tell, embarrassed by the thought that such secrets in their working methods might ever be discovered. Others, such as Byrd and Brahms, would feel that the skills of precise counterpoint are valuable as technical exercises but usually need to become more fluid for the sake of musical expressivity of the composition. Contrapuntalists, from medieval composers and their puzzle canons, through Bach to Webern, would agree that strict, tidy schemes have their place as *part* of the compositional endeavour. And the same could be said of composers who ensure that different sections of a piece are identical in length, as can be seen in various late works of Beethoven or Webern.

Composers have occasionally enjoyed the challenge of writing pieces, or sections of pieces, that reverse their direction at the halfway point – palindromes. Examples by Byrd or Haydn are clever but in fact demonstrate the limitations of this procedure, partly because the architectural halfway point is rarely the best dramatic turning point, but also because a truly cadential ending, in such styles, is not ideally a mere reverse of the chord sequence heard at the beginning. Items from Bach's *The Art of Fugue* and *A Musical Offering* transcend such considerations in their own unique way, and much the same could be said of a purist serial piece such as Nono's *Canti per Tredici*, firmly entrenched as it is in the 1950s avant-garde. Webern was a master of palindromic structures. These are very concentrated and refined, and as such achieve their own brand of classicism; but they are rarely exactly palindromic, since dynamics, flexibility of tempo, and timbre (the piano's attack-decay, for instance) are not reversed. Of the various examples in Berg, the most striking is the orchestral 'Film Scene' *Ostinato* in his opera *Lulu*, since this point in the work – the central scene in the central Act – is a literal turning-point in the drama and fully justifies both its place in the scheme and its palindromic process.

Composers have hinted at palindromic events within larger structures, in order to give added coherence. Take two examples: Part 2 of Bach's *St John Passion*, in which four choruses, Nos 29, 34, 36 and 38, return in approximately reverse order in Nos 42, 44, 50 and 46; and similar palindromic correspondences are to be found in Brahms's *Variations on a theme of Handel*, Op. 24, in that, of the 25 variations, Nos 5 and 21 are in the minor mode and 7 and 19 feature reiterated Fs, and so on. An example of a palindromic tonal scheme, as original and effective as it is unregarded, is found in the first movement of Schubert's Tenth Symphony, in which the first subject explores a tonal descent of D–C–B♭, to be answered in reverse in part of the second subject (B♭–C–D in the recapitulation).

As regards 'progressive tonality', in which a strict succession of keys is pursued as though pre-compositionally planned, we should recognize the occasional bold experiment for what it is, for example Bull's *Ut, re, me, fa, sol, la*,[13] in which all 12 major keys are employed (and some strange modulations too!). More important for my own music, from very early on, is the beautiful slow movement of Rawsthorne's First Piano Concerto, where a chaconne basis is set up in which each eight-bar section is a semitone higher. The effect is enhanced by the fact that the harmonic pattern itself tends towards a *downwards* direction.[14] The opening eight-bar section is given in Example 6.9.

Example 6.9   Alan Rawsthorne, First Piano Concerto, opening of second movement

Around this, for a few sections, melodic lines open up and textures become elaborated.[15] The possibilities inherent in such progressive tonality have remained with me, and my *Sonata-Rondo* is but one of many examples of its application.

Almost as a footnote, I feel tempted to cite a very different example of this process – the second movement of Schubert's *Trout* Quintet. I had often been struck by the extraordinary juxtaposition of G major and A flat major at the halfway point: a long drawn-out cadence settling gently into G, followed, with no hint of any transition, by the next phrase beginning a semitone higher. Neither key appears before or after this (see Example 6.10).

Why do we accept this as beautiful, even logical, rather than merely experimental or possibly miscalculated? The answer, I would suggest, lies in progressive tonality, which (even if we are not aware of it) is at work throughout the movement, as shown in Example 6.11.

The tonic of F moves through F# (minor, facilitated by the common 3rd degree) to G (the central cadence); the opening process is repeated in A♭ moving to A minor, from which the comforts of home suddenly appear in sight. (Again,

Example 6.10   Schubert, *Trout* Quintet, second movement, central cadence

as in the Rawsthorne, the whole journey of an octave is considered too much of a good thing.)

At this stage is would be reasonable to entertain the possibility that to divide the process of our musical experience of a work into the two clear stages (see page 87) would be unrealistically dogmatic. A little part of the second stage (awareness leading to identification) enters pretty soon, if our listening is a sufficiently developed skill and is sufficiently well disposed towards the work in question. But when talking about any music in detail (or any art, for that matter), especially if it is a work of one's own, one needs to be careful about when to divulge what, so that an awareness of structure can be led on the right path towards a deeper grasp, that 'true participation' of which Gerhard speaks. As composers, we all long for this extent of identification in our listeners and are deeply gratified on those rare occasions when we get it.

Example 6.10   continued

Example 6.11   Schubert, *Trout* Quintet, tonal plan of second movement

Notes

1 Peter Evans on the sleeve note to the LP of my First String Quartet (London: Argo, 1970).
2 This chapter was originally presented as part of the conference 'British Music in the 1990s' held at Roehampton in February 1999, and it followed the morning after the evening recital in which Dr O'Hagan performed *Sonata-Rondo*.
3 For a fuller discussion of this concept, see N. Cook, *Music, Imagination and Culture*, Oxford: OUP, 1990, pp. 10–22. In particular, consider his point that there is '... a widespread consensus of opinion among twentieth-century aestheticians and critics that listening to music is or, at any rate should be, a higher-order mental activity which combines sensory perception with a rational understanding based on some kind of knowledge of musical structure.' (Ibid. p. 21.)
4 Nicholas Cook, *BBC Music Magazine* (May 1999).
5 Graham George, *Tonality and Musical Structure* (London: Faber & Faber 1970), p. 30.
6 Roberto Gerhard, sleeve note to his Symphony No. 1 (London: EMI 'music today', 1965).
7 H. Keller *Essays on Music*, ed. C. Wintle, Cambridge, CUP, 1994. See Introduction, p. xx (quoted from 'Education and its Discontents', *The Listener*, No. 81/2080, 6 February 1969, p. 185, and No. 81/2089, 10 April 1969, p. 504).
8 This was in my talk for BBC Radio 3 (31 January 1973), in which I introduced the first broadcast performance of my *Symphony in Two Movements*.
9 Jana Frenklova, Powis Hall, University College of Wales, Bangor, 31 October 1996. The note's indicated duration of 'a little less than 15 minutes' has proved ambitious or idealistic: so far, performances have been around 16–17 minutes.
10 The score is available from the British Music Information Centre in London and the Scottish Music Information Centre in Glasgow. Plans are afoot for a CD recording, but so far the only impression of its sound-world that is publicly available is a 2-minute extract on my website – <www.sebastianforbes.com>.
11 Compare the maps of the London Underground published in 1924 and 1931: the earlier one is more accurate but far less informative, whereas the later one (which is essentially the one still used today) sacrifices strict accuracy for clarity.
12 In general, my choral music regards key centres a little more obviously, but the principle of progressive tonality often applies, one example being the Evening Canticles *Aedis Christi 1*. Strophic texts readily invite such treatment, as in the *Ely Carol* section from my *Hymn to St Etheldreda* (available on CD from Herald).
13 Fitzwilliam Virginal Book, No. 51.
14 In the event, the progressive tonal plan is interrupted and curtailed long before it completes its full course, Rawsthorne not being a composer given to completeness for its own sake.
15 A strictly repetitive descending bass line as a framework for expressive music can be traced back to Monteverdi's *Lamento della ninfa* and perhaps finds its climax in 'Dido's Lament' from Purcell's opera *Dido and Aeneas*.

PART II
INTERVIEWS

Chapter 7

A Conversation with Harrison Birtwistle

Robert Adlington

I met with Harrison Birtwistle in early February 2000. Our main topic of conversation was the Nine Movements for String Quartet, but we also touched upon other recent works. Birtwistle had been working that week on settings of the poetry of Lorinne Niedecker for soprano and cello, and he referred to them more than once in the course of our discussion. *The Last Supper* had also been recently completed – 'every last note', as the composer commented with evident relish. An informal parting exchange on this latest music theatre work revealed that it promised a move away from the relative conventionality of *The Second Mrs Kong*: Birtwistle was keen to point out that, in contrast to *Gawain* and *Mrs Kong*, he had avoided calling the work an opera, preferring instead the label 'dramatic tableaux'. One of the respects in which the piece differs from these earlier works of the 1990s is in its treatment of the performing space. By placing loudspeakers around the whole auditorium, so that sound is projected at the audience from all sides, and by bringing individual instrumentalists up out of the orchestral pit to comment upon the action from the edges of the stage, *The Last Supper* reintroduces into the theatre the sort of rethinking of performance configurations that is so characteristic of Birtwistle's instrumental music.

Instrumentation and instrumental layouts formed a recurrent theme in our discussion of the quartet movements. The relative lack of opportunity for instrumental theatre afforded by the string quartet may appear incongruous in the context of the rest of Birtwistle's output, but what emerged from our conversation was an underlying consistency of approach that treated the quality of an instrumental ensemble as a – or possibly the – primary point of departure for composition. This is manifest at the level of general conception, in Birtwistle's distinction between ensembles that have the quality of 'found objects' (the string quartet, or *Entr'actes and Sappho Fragments'* flute, viola and harp) and those that comprise more heterogeneous gatherings (for example, the wind quintet of *Five Distances*), and at the level of local detail, as is made clear by his revealing declaration of the centrality of the physicality of particular instruments, and their technique, for his writing. Thus it is that the instrumentation of *Five Distances* implied a certain overtly dramatic musical discourse, whereas the string quartet is treated almost as a single instrument, a neutral medium for the exploration of the minutiae of Birtwistle's compositional technique. (In this light, the occasional soloistic status of the viola may be understood in terms of the contaminating influence upon the

2   Harrison Birtwistle

cycle of the first Celan setting, 'White and Light' – where the viola acts as a nervous textural anchor – rather than as an expression of a theatrical potential inherent in the medium itself.)

We began with more general matters, however. Taking a cue from the title of the present volume, it seemed appropriate to enquire whether Birtwistle might view his own music of the 1990s as in any sense distinct from his earlier output.

RA: Do you view your output in terms of periods of stylistic uniformity, so that there are periods when you are doing one thing and periods when you are doing something else?

HB: Well that's for you to decide! My feeling is that I've got something in here [points to head] which is the same as it always was, and that it's a sort of evolutionary thing rather than that I come to a crossroads or a watershed – I've never felt that, ever. The journey from one thing to the other usually happens *within* a piece. You know, I see possibilities where I am ... and also in a lot of cases I'm trying to find a way back ...

RA: I find it difficult, looking at your work-list, to chunk it off into periods – you know, those works are 'early Birtwistle' and they're concerned with x, y and z, and those later works are concerned with something else. You seem to be dealing with a lot of things all the time.

HB: A lot of it's to do with memory. It's like it's all in the bag, and ... the devices are something which simply help me realize the ideas.

RA: Is the process of moving from one piece to the next usually a matter of wanting to pick up the same sort of problems, or more a matter of wanting to deal with different ones – or is it a mixture?

HB: I think it's a mixture, because ... I don't know whether what you think I do is a sort of schizophrenic thing. These songs are a pretty good example, actually. They're lyrical and very fragile – they hardly raise their voice. I'm trying to make the scale of the music correspond to the scale of those little verses. So there's that sort of thing. But then I plan to write next a piece for piano and percussion which is like the world of my piano pieces, but even more so! So sometimes you mix all these things together, and at other times you lay them out more separately ... You know, I don't think any of the fragile aspect is going to come into this piece for piano and percussion. I'm sure it's not – not in that sense, anyway. I mean it might be quiet and fluttery in places, but not quiet in the same way ...

RA: I always think of *The Cry of Anubis* and *Panic*: they're more or less adjacent pieces in your output yet could hardly be more different ...

HB: Yes ... I hadn't thought of that, that's right. But then again, if you take *Pulse Shadows*, there's an idea of trying to do something like this [interlocks spread fingers of both hands], where each part has its own individual coherence like a comb [holds hands separately] – the songs or the string quartets – but also a logical variety. And then when interlarding them, there are things that unify them, across the separate groups. So you separate them, and there's variety and contrast in each part, and you put them together and ... it's sort of an illusion. It's also throwing things together which don't necessarily correspond. As you know, in *Secret Theatre*, there's a thing up here, and a thing down here [gestures] – they're in a permanent state of collision, yet there is unity between them because I know how the pitches work. And yet at the same time, one's conceived horizontally and one's conceived vertically. The same idea's in the Celan cycle. At one time I thought that I could just have a sheaf of pieces that you could play any number of, in any order. But then I started considering how I wanted them to go together ...

RA: The score says that they can be played in almost any selection or order – do you now feel that that wouldn't necessarily work?

HB: Oh, I don't know ... Well, I think that works alright once you've separated the songs and the quartets out. But then the string quartets are arranged fairly much 'fast–slow–fast–slow', so there *is* a sort of logic there.

RA: I remember thinking as the cycle of quartets started evolving that the string quartet doesn't seem an obvious medium for you – because it's a relatively homogeneous ensemble, which doesn't hold obvious potential for instrumental roles or instrumental theatre in the way that a wind quintet might. In fact I find it difficult to think of another ensemble piece of yours that doesn't afford those sort of possibilities for instrumental theatre. I know that in some of the pieces the viola strikes out by itself ...

HB: Well initially I thought that the viola was going to have a particular role, but it disappeared. The role sort of ... it's like somebody coming out of a crowd, and you see them at the front, but then they disappear ... or like someone in a play, where it seems at the beginning of the play that they're going to be important and yet it turns out that they're not. And I like that.

RA: There are just three of the pieces, I think, where the viola is scurrying round by itself.

HB: Yes, that's right, it does that. But it's very shadowy. It's not something which I was constantly thinking about.

RA: Would you say that that's something different about these pieces, compared to earlier ensemble works? You don't even ask the quartet to be set up differently, they're just sitting in the conventional arrangement.

HB: Well I sort of see the quartet as a found object. In *Tragoedia* they're a sort of found object too, although there you separate out the cello ... I think what the quartet pieces might be related to is *Entr'actes and Sappho Fragments*. I think there's something there – you get the songs and the instrumental music, and then the recomposition of the original material ...

RA: So there's a parallel in the treatment of the ensemble as well as in the inter-locking movements ...

HB: Yes, there's a source for the flute, viola and harp, which is the Debussy – so that's a sort of found object. And also in *Entr'actes and Sappho Fragments*, the idea of the piece beginning again is quite interesting – the piece still makes sense if you begin it at the moment the whole ensemble and the voice comes in; it's as if that's the proper beginning ...

RA: That's another similarity with the quartet movements. There are some very close correspondences between some of the quartet movements, to the extent that it is almost as if the cycle is being 'begun again' only in a different way.

HB: Yes, that's right.

RA: In some of your other music the idea of instrumental roles is often visually articulated in some way – either the instrumentalists are required to move around the stage, or are positioned in unorthodox ways. How important is it to be able to *see* your music, and what status does a sound recording have?

HB: Well I go with Stockhausen on this. Stockhausen says that recordings are like reproductions of pictures. In that sense they aren't the real thing.

RA: I'm thinking of a particular piece actually – *Five Distances* for wind quintet. There's something exciting about watching the instrumentalists cue one another which is not captured on the recording. When you're writing music, are those kind of visual elements integral to the process of composition or more something that you add later on?

HB: No, it underlies the whole process. The thing about the wind quintet is that it doesn't have any classical precedents. And it's the opposite to the string quartet in that all the instruments are different. The instrument that is really the odd ... the 'odd man out' – I don't know if it's politically correct to talk about that, but you know what I mean! – is the horn. The oboe and the bassoon are the same, and the flute and the clarinet also pair off together. And so consequently you set them in a position, not as a homogeneous group, but as a disparate group of instruments. The horn then has a function which is different to the others – like the horn in *Tragoedia*. And the instruments sitting next to each other on either side have a different relationship from the pairs sitting opposite each other: the two who are next to each other play accurately together, whereas the two opposite have a freer relationship. The horn acts as the time-keeper, because when they do play together he gives them a rhythmic cue, and that's like going ... [conducts a cue]. So in that sense, that's where form started in that piece – with the arrangement of the instruments.

RA: I was looking in Michael Hall's book, and he'd looked at the sketches for the first quartet movement, Frieze 1. He found something to do with open strings – that open strings seemed to be the point of departure for the composition ...

HB: Did he? That's interesting. Well you know what that's about – it's not really knowing how to write for a string instrument! I work it out from the open strings, knowing that that's ... I hadn't read that ...

RA: It's in Frieze 1 where there are little semiquaver figures that oscillate around different open strings in each of the instruments. Was that simply a point of departure, or more to do with getting a particular kind of sound? It certainly gives the quartet a more resonant sound ...

HB: Yeah, I like the open strings. It's funny you mention that because that's what I've been doing with the cello part in these songs. It also gets you out of a jam, though, because you know there's an open string and it's got a certain ... ease. I can't write music which I don't understand physically – that vibrates here [hand on chest] ... you know, if I don't know what it's like to play. I was a performer, and I know what a phrase is – what it's like to breathe a phrase. And if I don't get a sense of anything like that, I can't write it.

RA: You talked about this idea of the quartet as a found object. That connects to something I wanted to ask about your fugue. I don't know if I'm stating the obvious here, but Michael Hamburger in his introduction to the Celan poems talks about the 'Todesfuge' as a 'gross fugue', in that it's dealing with such black, bleak matters – and then I suddenly thought of Beethoven's *Grosse Fuge*. It seems to me that your fugue is very much in the same world ...

HB: It's tampering with the Gods! You know, it's this incredible poem that you can hardly speak. I think you can say the same for all Celan's work – after the Holocaust, there isn't speech any more, you can't be a poet. So what he did in some respects is that you get these glimpses of fragments of a sort of language, a bit like digging things out of the ground. And the fugue is also a bit like a found object. I simply played a game with myself, of what I remembered a fugue was. It's a double fugue, and it's really only an exposition. I didn't want to go through all the paraphernalia of working it out as if it were some academic exercise. It's there in the title – fugue; it's something that's 'given'.

RA: Do you know the Beethoven?

HB: Yes of course I do. I don't know that there's any similarity.

RA: The bit that struck me the most is towards the end of yours all the instruments play the theme in unison, and of course the same happens in the Beethoven. Also the strenuousness of the music makes both pieces seem as if they're at the edge of possibility ...

HB: Yes, that's right. Also, in mine each instrument has its own subject, in a way. And then there's a sort of ghost element – I called it a 'ghost subject', which is very high. So it's really a three-dimensional thing – it's got five elements. It's playing with something ... I don't really know whether it's a fugue or not. But there is that bleakness. It's about black things.

RA: The concept of 'frieze' is important to the cycle, and there are perhaps two levels at which it can apply. You can talk about the whole cycle as a frieze, in the sense that it's made up of these little modules which are almost static situations but taken together add up to something bigger. But you're using the title for specific pieces as well ...

HB: Yes, because there are movements called Fantasias, which are through-composed and have a sort of logic – a beginning, a middle, and so on. Whereas the implication with the Friezes is that they're presenting something that goes on and on. It's a mechanism that doesn't have a logical beginning; I sort of have to 'fake' a beginning. They're also about these little ostinato figures, where you never hear the complete one. It's as if I made this thing [holds up hand] and then I chip different bits off every time it appears ...

RA: So there's no original ...

HB: Well there is, but it's accumulated.

RA: The frieze idea has something to do with staticity, but also with narrative – a narrative through that staticity. There's a sort of paradox ...

HB: There is a paradox, yes. You get movement as well, it 'carries' you. I mean, they go round rooms don't they? You end up where you started. I think the point about them is that they're conceptually different from the Fantasias. Also, going back to the question of the string quartet as being this found object: the instrumentation of the songs was given to me by John Woolrich, so even that was not my decision. I like the fact that there are instruments in common between the two ensembles. Then you get the bass instrument, the contra-bass, which is a sort of extension of the string quartet; and the clarinet, which has affinities with Mozart – that sort of dark texture.

RA: It's a wonderful ensemble ...

HB: Yes, it's a very good ensemble isn't it? So in a sense the whole piece was a question of accidents. The reason why I wrote the first song was an accident, and the reason why I wrote the first string quartet was an accident. They also demonstrate this thing I talked about earlier, with regard to the cello songs and the piano and percussion piece, in that they were two very different pieces. 'White and Light' is lyrical, and has the viola as a distinct voice; and then I wrote the second string quartet movement which is very ... [gestures furiously]. So there's a sort of opposite. Also, I didn't know who Celan was. I found him by accident ... It was the only poem I had in the house – I'd moved to a house in France – and I remember thinking, well this is wonderful. So it wasn't as if I sat down in a mystic haze one day and thought this is a fantastic idea ...

RA: No, because initially the cycles were quite separate weren't they, and then it was only later that they fused ...

HB: Yes. Well, it began very quickly after that. But when I was writing the string quartets, I always thought that I was writing the first one. Every time I wrote one I thought, you know, this will be good for the beginning! So they're all beginnings ...

RA: Though in the end the first Fantasia is so decisively a beginning ...

HB: Yeah, I think in the end I did write that as a beginning. Because, you know, the Celan songs are so much to do with darkness, that I didn't want to begin with atmosphere – you know, as if to say 'here we are, very serious'. I sort of saw the opening as like a dark Monteverdi. Like the Vespers: a sort of fanfare, that brings you into it. It's a bit like injecting something: that's the thing that breaks through the skin, and then it disintegrates after the opening ...

RA: It is very statuesque that beginning – in the Vespers as well. It's a fanfare, but it's also almost like a set of columns ...

HB: That's right. I think that's the sort of thing I had in mind.

Chapter 8

An Interview with Jonathan Harvey

Julian Johnson

JJ: How would you describe the directions your music took during the 1990s?

JH: The 1990s really began with a continuation of the 1980s, with *Ritual Melodies*. This used quite strict techniques of making melodies which were ambiguous but memorable – melodies that made polyphonic combinations of, for instance, melody A and melody B, and a third melody 'A+B', and then they could be used as long chains of 'modulations' so that the intervals between melodies could be composed with. *Ritual Melodies* was started in 1985 but was finished in 1990. So in some of those works of the late 1980s I was using that same formal search for rigour – of being able to remember things over long periods of time and also to recognize them in dense polyphonies. I was very struck by Messiaen's bird song and by how you could recognize anything from three to fifteen different birds at the same time – how you could recognize consistent differences in the polyphony, which wasn't just a mass texture but had real characters in it ... as Mozart, for instance, was achieving in the *Jupiter* stretto and Schoenberg was achieving in parts of the First Chamber Symphony ... many well-defined themes occurring in combination. That was the sort of thing I was after rather than fugal texture, which is in general just the same idea in different voices. Alright, the same idea is recognized but it's not so exciting as the tension between *different* ideas recognized simultaneously. Depth and ambiguity was the point of that. To make things belong to different identities. There's the melody with the dotted rhythm identity and there's the one with the trill identity and a composite theme which had both – neither one nor the other. Because the shape 'added up' there would be something which was completely individual about the latter, I hoped, something personal only to itself. And that went into the opera which I was writing all that time – I started it in 1989 and finished in May 1992. It also used the chain of melodies – one for each character or situation or passion in quite a Wagnerian way – and they made a chain which interlocked so the melodies could combine with each other and move through the harmonic fields. There would be the usual number of eight or so harmonic fields for the whole work and each melody would be composed in one field; but that didn't mean to say it couldn't be sieved through another field, in which case it would retain its rhythmic character but not its intervallic character.

JJ: How was that different to what you were doing earlier? What did you change to make these melodic materials more immediately recognizable?

3   Jonathan Harvey

JH: I had the 'courage', I think, to enjoy melodies and thematicism. It was again the old avant-garde taboo on thematicism. I remember one French composer in the 1980s proclaiming in his presentation: 'Melodies are dead for ever. We will never write any more themes!' I, who spoke next, said this is exactly the opposite of how I felt and I'm returning to melodies more and more as recognizable, useful things to build with. So it was really that. I think things changed after *Bhakti* (1982), which was actually quite a melodic work. *Bhakti* is my last 12-tone work and its series is a kind of Bergian melodic series which you can whistle and remember. But even so it was basically a cellular piece, working with Babbitt-like arrays and trichords, pentachords and tetrachords and so on. After that, after 1982, I began to move towards melodies. But I formalized it in 1985 with *Ritual Melodies*. And then most of the works of the next six to seven years used that kind of technique.

JJ: Does this interest in melody continue right through the 1990s?

JH: In some works it does continue. I think there's a great love of it which, now released, can't be put back into the bottle. The soprano I was working with in Vienna last week commented on how the music sings so gratefully and has a real feeling for line. Of course I was a singer, so I've allowed that to come out. I think the thing that has changed is really a search for naturalness – more and more. I can only put it like that. It's a love of Debussy and Debussy's forms – but the shorter pieces. Actually, a love of short music, of the short music of the atonal period of the Second Viennese School. A love of this sense of breaking out of everything –

the feel of a kind of liberation. And that's what I really want. Having worked very hard to learn a craft I want this feeling now of breaking out, of just doing nothing according to any rules I know. And that gives me the greatest pleasure – if I can do it.

JJ: Sometimes your music seems to work *towards* melody? As if melody is gradually formed out of more disparate initial elements?

JH: Sometimes, yes – in a work like *Scena* for example. That puts forward a melody fairly early on – a kind of folk melody with quarter-tones, just a whole tone and a kind of major-minor third. And it doesn't make a lot of it. It then becomes rather cellular and goes into the texture, but at the end it comes out as a very straight melody – in fact in unison. This is a work of metamorphosis definitely; it goes on a narrative journey and breaks out, I like to think. Again, it's this whole search for breaking out which fascinates me in art – psychologically I suppose. It's connected with Buddhism. The basic aim of Buddhism is to break out. You know the idea of the *koan* in Zen is to shatter every logical process in the mind: you break out and suddenly your eyes are opened and you see the world. It's just the same as before but you see it in a completely different light. That's what I mean by breaking out, and being close to Buddhism has given me rather a consciousness of this breaking out. Of course, very few human beings 'realize' it but its talked about a lot and I love the idea of the journey towards it – of a narrative. So a melody can be a kind of innocent, unburdened thing which comes as the goal of a journey, as representative of a breaking free.

JJ: The Cello Concerto often uses a more sustained, less fragmentary sense of melody. Is that related to your opera, *Inquest of Love*, with which it was contemporary?

JH: Well the Cello Concerto is based on the first part of the opera. It was written at the same time as the opera and uses some of the material from it. It was a coincidence of events. I'd started work on the opera and had written the first scene (which is very short, just an introduction) and got to the end of the subsequent duet. And then there was a fracas at English National Opera. David Pountney suddenly decided (quite rightly) that the libretto wouldn't do. He thought it would be much better to get another version made of the same idea. He liked the idea – nothing wrong with the basic concept – but he thought there were too many words and the expression was going to be too obscure – that the words were too poetic. And so he then asked David Rudkin to be my collaborator and the rest is history. But because of that there was a long gap of about nine months before any of the new libretto began to appear and I had a commission for a festival in Parma. So this coincided, and that's what I turned to do – but it wasn't very long to write a cello concerto – just nine months – and I decided that it would be rather good to use the material from the opera, because the cello is such a singing instrument, and then go on from a certain point to new material; again, trying to find this new Debussyan sense of form. I didn't want to plan anything. I wanted a great sense of improvisation ... a sense that the continuity has its own logic but I can't say why it has a logic. That kind of feeling. So having followed, in the first part, quite a thematic chain connected with the structure of the opera which was fairly tight, I didn't abandon those melodies but I used them very freely and improvisatorily for the rest of the work.

JJ: I was interested to read that you found it difficult to write some of the darker music of the opera. But in many of your recent works, such as *Death of Light/ Light of Death*, the *Wheel of Emptiness* or *Ashes Dance Back*, the music often seems to dwell on an all-consuming emptiness. Is that something you've explored only in your more recent music or has that always been there?

JH: I think that's always been there. The works of the 1960s and 1970s were often dark. Funnily enough the works called *Inner Light* (particularly *Inner Light 3*) were quite dark works. But the reason why the darkness is there is what I was touching on before – the love of narrative. The hero always has to have the adventure in the underworld and kill the monsters. Maybe it's that – I'm psychoanalysing myself here. I'm not really conscious of it. But I do know I don't want music which seems easily won: one no longer trusts art degraded by commercialism, the 'beautiful' picture on the chocolate box. Because, as I say at the end of my book, *Music and Inspiration*, where we're at now is confronting the whole range of human experience. I say *now* – it's obviously been the case since Freud and before the beginning of the twentieth century. But gradually throughout the decades the practice of putting evil aside and just dismissing it has crumbled as something which can't be contemplated any more and we have to reform everything by looking very seriously at what we are, in ultimate honesty, and it's not a pretty sight. Everybody is suffering without exception – unless in the rare case that they've achieved some kind of liberation. One of the exercises in Buddhism is to acknowledge that there is suffering. A lot of people push it away or they take an aspirin – they take a mental aspirin and say 'On no, I'm perfectly happy thank you. Nothing wrong with my life'. But our basic condition is a condition of suffering and if they really examine how they think of change they will find that although they may be temporarily happy they cannot really suffer change gladly. People want things to be permanent; we want to attach ourselves to things. We have a vision of the perfect afternoon or the perfect relationship or whatever and we persuade ourselves that it is real whereas in fact it's changing – and obviously the worst thing is that we get old and die. But I want to acknowledge that in art because I think only by acknowledging it can you achieve 'emptiness', the realization that things don't exist without our construction, which is actually the same as bliss. There's nothing dark about emptiness – it's a liberation from the self-grasping mind. It's actually an incredibly wonderful experience which one can glimpse but which is very hard to maintain. So I would say that my music is actually about bliss. (We must say what we think!) And the music is about that but it's by way of this difficult path of understanding the nature of suffering. It's like the quest for happiness that obsessed everyone in the eighteenth century. Many of the philosophers were asking 'What is happiness?' Well it's the same question: what is suffering? What is happiness? It's the same. But I see art as one of the great door-openers. Particularly music.

JJ: Of course, you have to do all this musically! If your music explores suffering and darkness but yet ends up as 'blissful', then the music itself is somehow involved in the transformation of one to the other. How do you shape musical sound to effect such a transformation?

JH: How to break out? For one thing you can simply set rules and break them, which is a little bit tame because *you've* set the rules and then you break them (but you could have set different rules which you didn't break in the process). However that is nevertheless a very strong *image*, if you set up a certain procedure and then you shatter it. Another way of course is to use the comparatively unknown world of electronics to break open the rules. I'm using these rules of creativity because I think they're very far-reaching psychological factors. We do think in terms of playing a game according to certain rules and in so much of what we do, even if it seems to be very free, we're usually obeying some rules. Much of this breaking out is a matter of trying to give the image – if not the experience, at least a *symbol* of breaking these rules. It's not something I can talk about because it's too artistic. It's a matter of sensing in a work how to do it differently each time. You ask for techniques: I would say electronics were probably the most common general technique I would use to make a complete change, but it could be a number of things – pitch or rhythm, for example. Also there is another technique which I want to push much further which is related to electronics and that is noise – or non-pitch, or half-pitch. I have a great desire to write a kind of music which hovers between pitch and non-pitch. White noise is an extreme example of it. It would be coloured noise, it would be the filtering of noise into quasi pitch-like structures and then broadening the filters so to speak so that one gets back to the loss of precise pitch. This kind of relation to the natural world – to the wind, to the sea, and so on – is fascinating. It's also fascinating in the sense of breaking out of the rules of classical music, where as a rule you have a well-defined pitch and you put in your rather feeble cymbal or tam-tam. That's not going very far. I want to take that direction much further in the future but I think it answers your question about the kind of technique that one can use to make transformations.

JJ: Do you think in general it has been harder for contemporary composers to break out in the way you describe – because it's hard to break the rules when all the rules seem broken?

JH: Yes. It's always the case, I think, that contemporary art is breaking rules all over the place of one sort or another and inevitably you have to seem to step back a little bit to establish rules if you're really going to shock with an explosion. That might be worth doing. I think Mahler did that. Much of his music seems to step back into a very simple style in order the more to articulate the length of the journey travelled. However, it's a matter of intuition. I set up the parameters of the work, the way it seems to make its coherence and that is contextual just to that work – it's not using a standard practice or language of the age, but it sets up rules of play to some extent and then proceeds from there.

JJ: Does what you've said about 'breaking out' come close to the idea of transcendence in music?

JH: I think transcendence is a very wonderful and inspiring word but fundamentally it means the same as what I'm talking about with 'breaking out'. I haven't used the word 'transcendent' for quite some time. It appears in my book *In Quest of Spirit* but I wrote that in 1995. I think more in terms of realization or liberation, which is a seeing-through of the illusory nature of our thinking – so that is transcending thought. It seems to me that it is really going beyond everything that ties us up, hems us around, keeps us in place, imprisons us. I'm not sure I can think of a more exact sense of transcendence, except in the way the term is used in transcendental meditation where one reaches a point in meditation of not-thinking, of pure awareness as some people call it, where you are thinking I suppose but it has a kind of purity, an innocence of concepts. But I think also it can be without anything, although often very brief. Whatever it is, it's hard to talk about: it's beyond words and you recognize it when you've been there. And that is called transcendence.

JJ: Your work *Advaya*, for example, seems to offer an image of transcendence in quite a literal way, in that the boundaries of what an acoustic cello can do are transcended by means of the electronic transformation of the cello's sound. I'm struck by your appetite for playing with these boundaries and with moving 'to and fro' across the middle ground.

JH: I'm interested in your use of 'fro'. We've been talking about 'to' quite a bit – going on a journey – but you're absolutely right, there's a lot of 'fro' as well, going over to something very different and then returning and trying to make that pathway clear. If the pathway is clear as one thing, not just as a linear direction but as an object which you can see both ends of and also the middle of, then it's a unity, it's a field which is visible at one glance. It's not just a journey where you can only see the beginning and an arrival where you can only see the end. I think the global view is more important than the journey – just to go in a line, which is a bit mono-dimensional. That is a more philosophical understanding. It's wiser to understand the totality rather than just the end result.

JJ: The experience of working with electronics has obviously changed your way of writing for instruments. You seem fascinated by the edges and limits of the sounds acoustic instruments can produce?

JH: Yes, that's right. Of course it is an image of breaking out or transcendence again. It shows, within a certain limited field – maybe the field of the violin or the string quartet – which is a symbolic field, a near breaking out, almost doing things you wouldn't think could be done within that field. Of course you can't do anything which *can't* be done within it, but it's a kind of image of that.

JJ: Is it very different for you writing a work without electronics, like the Percussion Concerto for example?

JH: It's quite hard to place that piece in the terms we've been talking about. It's more of a classical piece which only in the third movement seems to take on this spontaneous quality, perhaps also in the slow movement to some extent but it doesn't get very far, it rather dwells in one place and is a rather tranquil movement. But the first movement is fairly classical and very canonic. In the middle of the movement there is placed a kind of scherzo with slow movement – a mirror form in which the second half mirrors the first half. So it's very classical in structure. I was trying out canonic ideas which were fascinating me. Then the slow movement is a very static movement with sliding harmonies so the ambiguity and indistinction is there but it doesn't particularly break out of that in any directional sense. But I think the third movement does. This involves electronics very slightly. At the final climax you get the loudest moment of all which suddenly expands to something which should be quite a surprise for the audience because there is nothing to warn you that this is suddenly, mysteriously, going to become bigger with an expansion of the image by means of reverberation through widely spaced speakers. But it's true I do say that this is ad lib and needn't be done. So I think the point still remains that without electronics the piece at that point attempts to explode. It does get into a frenzy such as it's never experienced in its half hour up till then. It just really goes wild and very fast and ... that's an image of losing control, losing all rules. After that it just dies down like matter which has exhausted itself. It's rather a physical, energetic movement with constant rhythm and a constant fast energy. It was inspired – I can almost resort to cliché – by the beautiful light on the Pacific that one sees in California, the shimmering motion, fast motion but static throughout the movement. But then at the end it gets into a still faster motion and then all of that is broken out of, broken up. So it may not be so extreme in that case but it seems to be there doesn't it? You might be able to find works in which the breakthrough doesn't happen at all. I'm not always conscious of wanting to do it. It's not a principle at all in any way. But I am conscious of having a predilection for this type of process.

JJ: Your interest with crossing the boundaries or breaking out obviously involves not just sound materials themselves but also the question of musical form. Your music often denies the listener any solid musical substance to hang on to and seems to throw up fragments of material only to dissolve them away again. Nevertheless, a piece *is* a piece, with a beginning and an end. Technically, how is it possible to square this circle of writing a formless form?

JH: The idea of a 'formless form' is very interesting. It's intuitive. It's all part of my desire to be spontaneous and to get back, more and more, to a simple state, to childhood, to the spontaneity of the unfettered mind: this is always the goal. So there's an improvisational feel; but having taught form and analysis of form for 40 years I don't think I'm particularly naive about form: I push it into an intuitive mode and rely on it to do its work. This kind of improvisation, feeling my way

out, I hope gets a deeper logic; and if I do fragment things and make them pretty
ungraspable, it's so that some different type of form will emerge which is rather
new or unfettered – one that's come out of the work itself and is not in any way
pre-planned or composed. *Wheel of Emptiness* is possibly a work you might
think of here. It's quite chaotic to start with ... well not exactly chaotic because
it's based on a series of 11 waves, each of which is a different compressed spectrum. So we're really going through a process of compressed spectra and that
works as a background form. Of course, one always uses certain things as pre-
planned devices but I don't deceive myself that they give a strong sense of form
per se. Anyway I go through these different densities of microtonal harmonic
fields in each wave and then arrive at a kind of opposite concept which is the
objet sonore – using fifteen of these, scored for from one to fifteen instruments
and arranged in irregular but intuitive order. Each object is completely syntacti-
cally self-sufficient, there's nothing reaching out to any other object. An object is
composed of a note, or two or three notes, with some percussion often, some
noise element, a little glissando, a little quirk of some sort, but it's just an object.
So that's a kind of noticeable formal break; but within itself it may seem to be
chaotic because it has no through-flowing grammar. But as in the String Quartet
No. 2 where I likewise used 'found chords', constructed completely without any
relation to each other at all with crazy microtones and things, the process of
treating these isolated objects becomes a formal one because as the work
progresses they're actually made to lose this Cagean object-nature and to split
apart and decompose and begin to bleed into each other and become connected in
long lines as if they're melted down and made into something, like metal made
into a beautiful bowl. It may not be very obvious: it's not like ending up with a
simple melody, but that's the process anyway – that there is a deconstruction of
their separateness. And then of course the waves come back and they begin to
melt into the objects, so what were very separate become similar. The idea of
Wheel of Emptiness is a Buddhist one, where identity and separateness are seen
as an illusion rather clearly and everything is dissolved into the flow of change
which actually is the nature of the world. Everything changes. In a thousand
years, twenty thousand years, nothing that we see now will be remotely like what
we see it to be, and that's the kind of idea of the piece, that everything dissolves
and forms new forms.

JJ: That's an *idée fixe* perhaps of your music, that whole idea of showing things
to be insubstantial?

JH: Yes! Well actually I think that's the idea of music. That's the wonder of
music: ideas are proposed and then dissolved. If you just keep repeating the same
idea – how boring – it's just not a piece of music that one could listen to. The fact
that it does change however slightly means that to some extent it's beginning to
dissolve and become enigmatic and lose that definiteness you whistled.

JJ: More generally, what do you consider were the most significant developments
in music towards the end of the twentieth century?

JH: Electronics has obviously facilitated a whole range of new possibilities technically and it's really the most remarkable thing to have happened to music since the war. And of course computer development has been quite extraordinary. It's not always easy to point to the great works but as a great *possibility* I think it can't be denied that computer manipulation is so far-reaching that, for me, that has to be the number one candidate for how music has changed at the end of the twentieth century. I suppose a lot of people would disagree with it because most of our great composers don't touch it, with obvious exceptions, but for me there is no doubt. While electronics are a technical breakthrough I have called spectralism a spiritual breakthrough, which might be a little bit partial because it chimes in so well with my idea of showing the ambiguity of music, of how something can be a spectrum and also be a part or component of it. So it's both one individual thing and part of something at the same time. It's both a wave and a particle, in the terms of contemporary science. Some good books will have to be written quite soon about how art and science are really approaching each other at last, without opposition. People talk about scientific truth being objective, artistic truth being subjective. Of course, on a simple level that's obviously correct but in fact the two truths are beginning to come together in a way that can sensibly be discussed. Spectralism is a great leap forward towards finding a new grammar based on nature. Not all spectralists would agree with that emphasis although it is obviously connected with nature, but to me it seems to be important because of spectralism's relationship to the natural series and, in the system of compressed spectra by equal addition, you have something which obviously sticks pretty close to nature and can be clearly measurable against the natural series. What is natural and what is unnatural is a bigger question which I won't go into but I'm aware of. (When I say natural I mean natural in quite a naive sense: what is obviously natural and often encountered, the natural harmonic series). So it's a fundamental revolution and it's a strongly based one. Because it examines both the inner structure of music and is capable of extension in the outer world of song and dance and 'outer' articulation, it leads to the unification of the two worlds: the world of the computer – which I think of as basically the world of the microscope, looking in incredible detail at acoustic structure rather than formal structure – and the world of formal structure itself. So that's the importance of the future of this music. To make pieces which are easily understood by an ear which is used only to Stravinsky and the easier pieces of the Viennese school is, I suppose, quite difficult and may not rapidly gain understanding. Using microtones is still difficult not only for composers but also a large number of listeners – except of course we've been hearing microtones ever since the year dot in monody. The precision is the new thing; here these microtones are meant structurally rather than just emotionally, as an inflection to create an emotional affect. There's no division here between the structure, the Pythagorean nature of the microtonal interval, and the affective. One can be the other equally happily and, for my part, I like to dart in and out of the natural series – where you sing with normal intonation with your instrument or voice – and the precisely altered one where you seem to be inflecting suddenly, both systematically and affectively.

JJ: As far as your own work is concerned, does spectralism offer contemporary music a new, higher-level idea of consonance?

JH: Yes. I've felt a rebirth of the triad which I haven't really been able to contemplate until fairly recently. I'm quite happy writing the normal triadic formations now because it seems part of the world I'm working with, not suddenly leaping back to a different world. In the latest work, *White as Jasmine*, I use a couple of triads (D flat and D major) which are quite surprising. They are in a 'breaking out' place in the text and although they are not strictly an evolution of spectra either – there isn't a logical line from one to the other – I feel that because I've used spectra in the work they do belong nevertheless. It makes possible a kind of inclusiveness.

JJ: What's your perspective, given the time you spend abroad, on what is going on now in contemporary music?

JH: You do see very strongly, when you travel a lot, that we are an island here and that people's view of musical culture is very insular. They inevitably inflate everything British to the centre (which is characteristic of all islands) whereas if you meet the average continental musician he or she has a perspective of eight to ten countries and knows what's happening in all of them more or less, and travels easily from Holland to Italy and the countries all around – every month perhaps. Of course, most of us in this country don't do that so much. It's a very different perspective and the people who are regarded as gods here are ignored or perhaps not thought of very highly over there – though there are exceptions. Some of our British composers are among the best in the world, but not as many as some people think. That's a striking perspective and you get irritated to hear rather conservative people thinking they know everything and you realize that it's a very narrow knowledge that they have. There's a greater intensity in continental Europe than in this country, a sentiment that music matters as a matter of life and death to more people, that music is looked to as something to do with the deepest problems of culture and society and spirituality, in a quite widespread way – which is wonderful. I wouldn't say this applies in America, sadly. I know California best and it's a very multicultural society. You realize that European culture is just one element in many possibilities: to study Japanese or Chinese or Korean culture is equally valid and one could go just as profoundly into that as into the study of Beethoven and Stockhausen. But this tends to rather dangerously devalue everything.

JJ: And what about your most recent work?

JH: I've just finished the composition of my Millennium Cantata for this year's BBC Proms. It's called *Mothers shall not cry*, which is a quotation from a demonstration placard. It has a political tone and takes up the idea of suffering and mothers. It's entirely for female choir, and starts off just with names, names of people who have disappeared or perished in bombs or massacres or gas chambers

... a lot of them children, a lot of them women, certainly innocent people ... but it's just strings and strings of names. The inspiration really came from the Buddhist concept of *samsara* – and other traditions too – but it's very strong in the idea of *samsara*. The subject is the throngs of beings in *samsara*, which one continually prays for or tries to benefit, the endless beings in *samsara* which includes all animal life and other realms too, ghost realms, suffering beings. Endless, innumerable, unnameable throngs in *samsara* which the Buddha – everyone can become a Buddha, one must try to become a Buddha – vows to save, to help. And that's basically the aim of the work. Nothing if not ambitious! So we start with a portrayal of the names, a few representative names, about a hundred or so which are at first sung in melody garlands, respectfully I hope, trying to give them the homage that they're precious, that each one of them is worthy of commemoration and time. And in that mood it starts. *Mothers shall not cry* was a Taiwanese demonstration placard for disappeared people, which took place in Turkey ... but which could have been taken from anywhere in the world. And then the subject moves on to various sacred texts, mostly written by women, to do with motherhood and the healing of suffering in one way or another. It ends with a kind of ritual in which the male and female are balanced. So it's not a plea just for the redemption of the feminine, the divine feminine, but for a balancing of the elements in our personality. The patriarchal age is really over, I hope, with the last millennium, and the next millennium will have a new emphasis – a more balanced one ... more motherliness ... less of the conquering hero about it ... less of the power struggles.

Chapter 9

A Conversation with James Dillon

Keith Potter

KP: In 1990, in the course of a perhaps doomed attempt to relate your then current activities to postmodernist concerns, I suggested that your 1988 solo violin piece, *Del Cuarto Elemento*, 'gives the impression of confronting the whole "violin tradition" both "classical" and "popular" '.[1] But I at least felt that we might agree on this particular 'postmodernist' point, since you were willing to admit to 'trying quite deliberately to engage the violin, in this case, on its own terms in some quite vital sense'.

Your recent Violin Concerto – premiered at the BBC Promenade Concerts on 3 August 2000 by Thomas Zehetmair – would seem, some dozen years on, to take these issues further. I wonder if we could start by uncovering some of the thinking behind the gestation, as well as the eventual nature, of the new concerto. What connections, if any, has this thinking to that behind *Del Cuarto Elemento*?

JD: When I spoke of engaging with the violin, in *Del Cuarto*, I was referring to an interest in the linkage between the actual physical structure of the instrument and how this may define certain musical boundaries. By approaching things from this direction, there is a kind of double inscription: in scrutinizing the character of the instrument, modes of playing, and so on, I begin to derive a musical vocabulary.

One concern, if not the primary concern, was how to find a mode of writing which had a responsible relationship both to the electronic spheres and to the implications of communication technology. This may seem like a contradictory activity, but the allusive qualities of which Arnold Whittall speaks[2] are an integral part of that modality. Hearing is a fluid act; somewhere between silence and sound we reinvent the world.

KP: What is the nature of the connections – assuming there are some – between what you call the 'electronic spheres' and your concern with the physical properties of the violin?

JD: It might operate on two levels. First, at the analytical level, whereby I may take on board the research into how an instrument might be acoustically examined beyond the realms of immediate perception. Secondly, how one might, metaphorically or otherwise, integrate electronic processes such as attenuation, intermodulation, and so on, or post-electronic temporality, into the fabric of musical construction.

KP: Can you give examples of one or two of these electronic processes at work, whether metaphorically or more directly, in the Violin Concerto?

131

4   James Dillon

JD: Not really! Working with computers for 20 years, the artifice of fabrication (an accepted price of computer technology) has inevitably infected the strategies of composition, a certain 'feeling' arises from the technical apparatus. Since *Nine Rivers*, the correspondence between 'matter' and 'energy' in my work has become in some ways more promiscuous, or at least has taken a number of sub-routes. This I see as part of a wider strategy; my need for long-term projects is important here. A great deal of what I refer to is now operating at a conceptual level, bearing in mind the notion that language is not only a means of communication but also an integral part of reason itself, and conceptualization is an attempt 'to grasp' something.

It could be argued that the attempt to translate, for instance, 'electronic processes' into musical processes may be an example of simply transposing abstraction. In effect, however, it is concrete, and this is important. Nature for me is the primary source of reference; I am, though, extremely aware of what a loaded term 'nature' is. What I refer to is the relationship between the structure of something and the forces to which that structure may be subject. A part of our experience of nature is abstract anyway. For example, if one admires the beauty of ripple patterns on the sand, when analysed they are merely the result of the ebb and flow of the tide in combination with the loose molecular structure of the beach. An interest in electronic processes can be both negative and positive. From analysis to fabrication there is a kind of transubstantiation.

KP: What effect has your consideration of 'post-electronic temporality' had on the way in which the Violin Concerto unfolds?

JD: Musical form is a kind of growth process. If, however, one conceives of time as a set of fractured zones, then what becomes of this process of growth? In some ways, it may be seen as closer to filmic procedures. I wanted to some extent to play with the character of the solo violin. Its setting and re-setting suggested not a movement from one state to another, but a kind of floating point against which memory is constituted as a network of subjective interactions: what Joyce in *Finnegans Wake* calls a 'merry go raum'.

KP: What exactly are 'the implications of communication technology' in the Violin Concerto?

JD: None directly. I am referring to something wider and a by now diffuse influence. Nevertheless, the task for me has always been to seek out a language which does not act merely as a sign for ideas, but actually brings them into being through a kind of differentiation. Not a 'mimetic' act, but an essential action.

KP: Let's return to the Violin Concerto, and to how you put these ideas into practice there.

JD: I have written a great deal for string instruments since *Del Cuarto*, so it would be reasonable to say that much of this is now absorbed information. Leaving aside the quirky dandyism which has attached itself to the idea of a concerto in general, the line between hero, virtuoso, clown, angel or trickster in the face of insurmountable odds is a fine one, and certainly part of the fascination of the genre. However, beyond the playful transformation of identity – the question of how to balance a coherent musical ambition (within the circus ring) – the degree of interaction between soloist and ensemble in some ways provokes a confrontation with the soloist's own being. The relationship between obsessional behaviour, the ego, and how this might translate into matter, is dealt with more at the molecular level rather than at the level of some poetic psychology.

The question of how to move towards an image of performance that takes the breath away is a primary one. Whether the gesture plays a more central role in a work for soloist and ensemble, how much and what kind of interaction may take place – these are for me questions of density or mass versus point and line.

Scored as the Violin Concerto is, for large orchestra and in a single movement, these questions are partially answered in different ways. I have no interest in being consistent, only radical. And this may also encompass a certain alienation from the musical material; there will always be a degree of self-organization in a musical form. What I mean by that is that certain functional decisions begin to impose their own constraints. Here a principal aspect of the musical material is its fluidity. Is the structure in a process of being built, or in decay and ruination, a music where there is no assured ground?

The answer is, of course, both. Against the rhizome-like, a-centred space of the orchestral landscape and the gaze of the soloist lies the tension of a mysterious topography; figure–ground relationships only become clear as the actuality of meaning is suspended. At times, there is an interpenetration of soli-tutti material; and it is for me the function of the single gaze (in this case the solo violin) not only to orientate focus – to fix, if only for a moment – but it is (and perhaps here lies the potential drama of the concerto) also an enactment of a kind of ritualized alienation. The soloist moves restlessly through lyrical flights, humour, aggression, compassion, delirium; sometimes a line emerges from an intersection of colour and gesture, where the soloist may take on a more communal role by submerging himself or herself in the background. But in some ways these are retrospective observations.

This said, I began with concerns of form, concerns as it were imbued with some of the above observations, or intuitions. The important thing was that the space between soloist and orchestra remained porous. The work consists of a predetermined set of textures: ostinati, orbital motion, symmetrical rhythmic patterns, pitch implosions, and so on, types of 'pure states' which are initially arranged as a set of overlapping cycles of differing periodicities and densities. Some turn slowly and surface only occasionally, others appear more frequently. The phase difference between the cycles accounts for coincidence, simultaneities, distortions, and so on; and from the shattered elements of sequential time, new constellations emerge, the single movement concentrating, I hope, a fluidity of expression.

The actual 'framing' is predetermined at some point in the making; the tendency of the material may take one by surprise. And, in a certain way, development is an extension of that surprise. Contour, scale, proportion, and so on, grow from an assessment of the material, which comes from the so-called 'pure states'; what Nietszche has called 'seeking that spark of divinity from within'. An obvious departure is the 'explicit' use of pulse, but this has crept into my work over the last years.

KP: Why has pulse become more, as you put it, 'explicit' in your recent output?

JD: I should try to be clearer. If we take the distinction between so called 'striated time' and 'smooth time' as a conceptual frame, in 'striated' time, some regular (or irregular) pulse will control the musical events; in so-called 'smooth' time, there will be no discernable pulse controlling events. I became interested in the difference, and one way of accessing this difference was through superposition, in some ways an attempt to access the tension between what I have spoken of in the past as a musical state poised somewhere between order and disorder.[3] One variation of this idea is to split the notion of pulse itself into, for example, 'implicit' and 'explicit'; the difference between explicit and implicit pulse is critical. Implied pulse here operates against a state of transition and may function as a kind of silent grid for the rate of change.

If, however, one then imagines a music of continuous transition (foreground) where the grid, the beat, remains constant (background) and can clearly be felt as constant, as operating outside of any functionality, then a potential rhythm, an ebb and flow, between foreground and background begins to materialize. I distinguish this from metric modulation; these processes are not restricted to metre, but maintain a functional relationship to other parameters separately or simultaneously. What is created is a kind of phase-space where foreground activity independent from background organization creates an energy, another dimension.

I believe the most interesting feature of so called 'systems music'[4] was the connection its American proponents made between amplitudinal and frequency phase spaces. The least interesting for me was the grinding beat picked up by the minimalists. More recently, in works like *Via Sacra* for orchestra and the Violin Concerto, I have shifted the emphasis towards a clearer framing of material.

KP: Several matters seem relevant here. One is an aspect of the Violin Concerto which we've not so far mentioned, but which will be among the most immediately evident to the listener: the initial 'framing' of the structure by the most direct allusion – a word which we'll explore further in a moment – to Scottish folk music which I've ever heard in your compositions. Explicit pulse is, inevitably, one crucial dimension of this. Does the Violin Concerto represent, as it seems to me, a further stage of the penetration of folk-music allusions already at work in *Del Cuarto Elemento*? Or are the allusions at work in the concerto of a quite different order?

JD: I'm not so sure if penetration is the right term, although I do like the word. I would attribute the folk elements as having more to do with a certain 'openness' of structure.

During the early 1970s, to finance my private studies, I took a part-time lab technician's job at the Imperial College of Science and Technology, here in London. I was working in the High Energy Nuclear Physics Department on the new CERN project,[5] which was analysing the data from particle accelerator experiments in Switzerland and at Stanford. Basically they were looking for origins of life! The quark was discovered whilst I was there. As a consequence, I began to read a great deal about the so-called 'new physics': how any explanation of cosmology and the nature of reality, as we observe it, does not fragment the latter from consciousness as we experience it. Although in some ways I was highly sceptical about aspects of this scientific work, I was nevertheless intrigued that it set off certain resonances in my thinking about, for example, the nature/culture debate.

By a different route, and closer to my own studies into metaphysics, I was at the same time discovering French structuralist theories. A model thinker for the Structuralists was the Scottish morphologist D'Arcy Thompson. In the final chapter of his most famous book, *On Growth and Form*,[6] he demonstrates the connection between pattern and shape in nature through co-ordinate geometry, whereby through a sequence of ordered steps one shape may be transformed over time into another, usually out of some biological need for adaptation. What excited me at the time was that I was beginning to articulate, albeit in a rather modest way, my own sense that, for example, the nature/culture conflict was a functional expression of language; it was a question of polarity rather than opposition.

To return to your question. An integral part of the way I work is to organize things both according to their 'attributes' and their 'potential'. If one, for example, begins with two clearly defined and quite different pitch arrangements, and then transforms the first through a series of discrete steps into the second – rather like Thompson's co-ordinate transformations – this process would for me count as a stage in an 'open' structure. If I apply the same procedures to a set of musical scales or modes, then we begin to get closer to a kind of modulation. (Perhaps the greatest loss with the demise of functional tonality is the sensuality of key modulation.) I wanted every process or pattern to be in a continuous dance, a transaction where it could conduct or negotiate a performance with a continuously changing partner.

The meta-folk elements can be partly explained technically in that, through pitch substitution, it is possible to move in and out of different musical persona. So why folk elements? Well, I could explain these in terms of symbolism, aesthetics or semiotics; and, in some ways, perhaps allusion always contains its own reduction. There is, of course, a play with memory, and by memory I mean a transcendent memory beyond the immediately formal. But perhaps all music is a play with memory. The allusions are generally fleeting and in a state of flux; and like many of our experiences both intriguing and puzzling, folk music also has this innocent/experience quality that I like.

I should qualify this. At a time when all of the worst predictions about the commodification of music have materialized, it is in fact quite remarkable how, given the right conditions, certain nursery rhymes, folk melodies or simple rhythmic patterns can still cast a spell. There can also be a certain resistance to culturalization in some folk music to which I am attracted: for example, Mississipi delta blues. Or there can be a simple play with sound, the onomatopoeia of *puirt a beul* (mouth music) in Scotland, for example; this is the music of my grandmother, and my first contact with music.

Anyway, to return to 'fluidity'. One aspect of musical construction in which I began, in the late 1970s, to take an interest was timbre. I was particularly interested whether a deeper exploration of musical colour, an unstable parameter, might allow for more acute correspondences than the other parameters of a musical construction. This interest in timbre led to an examination of the relationship between 'spectral information' – I was familiar, of course, with works like Stockhausen's *Stimmung*, and later discovered the so-called French spectral school[7] – and 'frequency'. I was not so much interested in writing so called 'spectral music'; it was a question of finding a kind of connective tissue which could be organized independently.

A music which seems to be perpetuated by a sensation of season was an idea with which I played. However, I was aiming at something where nature was not always the primary source, but was locked in a cycle with more obviously mediated ideas: cultural sources. In the case of music, cultural sources are either 'compositional techniques' or they are 'referential'; they allude to an otherness.

In some ways herein lies the tension and the fluidity. Timbre seemed to offer conditions for the kind of movement I was seeking, or at least the gravity to which the material is subject. Not simply as a colourist; my concerns are a little more comprehensive than the senses. As Francis Bacon would say, 'it's the nervous system that interests me'.

KP: Another relevant consideration is what you call the Violin Concerto's 'predetermined set of textures'. These 'pure states', as you term them, include ostinati and rhythmic symmetries, so pulse clearly plays a significant role here. Have you recently found fresh ways of deploying the 'fluidity' of musical material which you've said is so important to you, so as to incorporate, say, greater audible regularity?

JD: I think in more recent work I have stripped away much of the surface activity and allowed for a coarser unfolding. It's more a question of emphasis than difference. I am still exploring forms of energy, the borders of material expression; and the allusive qualities that may lie therein have moved perhaps more to the foreground. Sometimes it is simply a question of exhaustion; that I need to see afresh what I'm doing.

There are a number of reasons for shifting the emphasis, and perhaps part of that has something to do with playfulness, the 'delight' of making. The juxtapositions of material in recent works are deliberately stark. The interpenetrating resonance fields of *helle Nacht* have been sacrificed for the bare parallel bands of volumes and planes in the Violin Concerto.

There are two fundamental kinds of musical space: the interior sensual space of detail, and an exterior, meditative space without apparent boundaries. It is the first of these spaces which has to some extent been sacrificed in the concerto. The detail within the massed textures is less dense to allow the soloist to speak.

KP: I'm fascinated to learn more of what you meant when you said that you 'have no interest in being consistent, only radical'.

JD: Oh! I suppose one of the most persistent comments I have had made to me in recent years is that it is impossible to second-guess where I might go next. Why this should be an interesting activity I can't imagine; much too much is made of this. I have always maintained a right to be, in the words of Cezanne, 'innocent' when confronted with the expectations of others. Consistency says little about coherence; one can be blindly foolish and extremely consistent.

Of course, 'radical' has political as well as philosophical overtones – and I don't mean the farce of political systems. I'm aware that there is a social dimension to what I do; the 'social' has to do with maintaining something. The recent nonsensical diversion about elitism in Britain, for example, seemed to me to be a ploy to distract attention away from 'privilege', and how privilege has little to offer in the defence of a living tradition, and a great deal to protect in the culture industry. The question of tradition for me is something to do with knowing yourself and, more importantly, this demands knowing something about otherness.

Adorno's idea of a radical language, a progressive musical technique, does not go far enough, since it restricts itself to the realms of politics and aesthetics. And whilst I may concur with his notion of liquifying the aura of the music industry, it says little about the actuality of musical energy. Of course, all musical action demands energy; the commencement of any sound is characterized by a starting transient, a fleeting attack to put it into time – a short concentration of energy. One law of nature is that all movement must have energy, and all natural systems decay when there is a lack of energy.

In some ways, this can be seen as a metaphor for post-industrial music. A progressive technique, for me, must also engage with the actuality of sound, and how this might philosophically impact on both the politics and the practice of music. The reduction of sound is a consequence of the industrialization of technical and performance practices in the conservatoires, the electrical degeneration of sound, and a cynical promotion of the mediocre by the recording industry.

I have never had much time for the 'style wars', which are simply another diversion. Arguments about style – serialism versus tonality, maximalism versus minimalism, and so on – were discredited long before I began to make music, and have long been the blunt tool of the neo-conservatives. A music of high energy must not, of necessity, be associated with a crude gestural language; this rarely amounts to more than montage. In fact, high energy will often defy its own gravity, will turn towards the essence of movement and create a certain stillness. Malraux says that 'it is not emotion that destroys a work, but the desire to demonstrate something'.[8]

Instead, I refer to something that is operative at both low and high levels of a composition. The quality of sound resonance is a mirror of form. The convergence of levels is what I mean by high energy; it's a question of luminosity. The idea of the 'speculum' is central; Joyce's definition of modern art, recalling Hamlet, as a 'cracked glass' is more a reminder of fragility than a definition of art. Any connection between complexity and radicalism must exclude style, and has to do with otherness. A part of that otherness is a refusal fully (or is it 'fooly'?) to participate in the strictures of a vulgarity which tries to equate style with meaning, and consistency with knowledge.

KP: Doesn't all this suggest considerations worlds away from the kind of 'allusions' to which Whittall refers in his conference paper, when analysing your Third String Quartet?

JD: On the contrary, since it is depth of which I am speaking. And if form is capable of a rich and endless ambiguity, then the allusive nature of musical relationships will be an inevitable part of a musical work. What interests me is something that hovers around the substance of a work. Rilke spoke of 'a blue that is unsupported anywhere'.[9]

KP: Yet Whittall's references to 'allusion' in the Third String Quartet are quite specific.[10] He refers, for instance, to the way in which the 'homophonic reiteration' of middle D, in your quartet's second movement, is used as 'a force to constrain and even suppress attempts at melodic, decorative dispersal'; and he suggests comparisons with the similarly 'rhythmically brittle way' in which Bartók stresses Ds for a similar purpose in the middle movement of his Second Quartet.

Whittall acknowledges that 'Sensing some similarity in this matter is very much the small change of critical reception'. But he argues that 'because it serves more to distance Dillon from Bartók than to demonstrate an abject, fearful dependency, it can open up a whole treasure chest of analytical enterprises'. It also, he avers, 'shows that the possibility of allusion to a certain number of structural and stylistic associations is one way in which the composer can contribute something personal to the string quartet genre: and that without needing to be completely and irrevocably separated off from the quartet tradition'.

Were any connections to such Bartókian strategies of conscious concern to you in the composition of your Third Quartet? And whether they were or not, what are your reactions to this particular comparison? And to such comparisons more generally, if they are made with the sort of serious analytical scrutiny which Whittall brings to them?

JD: Arnold's perceptions are exactly that, and I have no reaction beyond a certain sense of gratitude that they arise from a point of integrity. His concerns lay outside of mine. The difference is crucial and takes us as close as anything to a reasonable sense of the untranslatable. There was no conscious attempt to adopt 'Bartókian strategies' to my ends.

KP: Whether they are 'Bartókian strategies' or whatever, I can't help being fascinated, for instance, by the later stages of the Third Quartet's third movement. After the rather complex 'fall-out' from this movement's initial, grinding secundal dissonances, we suddenly get a sequence of passages in which some kind of modality plays a significant role: the 'impressionist' tremolandi of bars 61–2, the ensuing, much longer, passage of trills. Although these aren't as 'white-note' as they look at a glance on the page, the rhythmic repetition and fairly static aspect of the pitch gamut here – at least before it unravels further from bar 75 onwards – make for a music which, to me, is very much built around pitch centricities and the tantalizing suggestion of 'allusion'.

JD: The passage to which you refer reaches a point where rupture is no longer an option. Much of the structure has to do with a kind of entropy. Each movement begins with an idea which is gradually put under strain. Already by bar 53, there is a question mark. And at bar 61, I open a window: it's that shock of light, suddenly everything has a different meaning. At bar 63, we are abruptly confronted with the possibility that we are listening with the wrong ears; and yet, almost immediately, entropy again sets in.

KP: To conclude, I'd like to ask you to clarify and contextualize some aspects of our earlier discussion. If both an essentially radical approach and folk music have long been components of your compositional stance, does this represent simply a dualism or a more complex, consciously driven dialectic? And has the balance between these components really not shifted away from radicalism as such during your output of the 1990s?

JD: First of all, I don't make quite the same distinctions and, secondly, things have to be viewed over a longer period. It is not simply a question of dividing material up according to its identity. All materials, whether of a quasi-folk nature or more complex, are elements in a larger transformation. Everything is reflected in everything else.

It's rather like the relationship between arithmetic and mathematics: one is imbued with the other. What connects things is the technical imagination, and focusing on the theme. Part of the attraction is that there is no balance. To paraphrase Oedipus, it's all about bringing dark things into light. There will always be a certain conceit and concealment involved; it has little to do with folk music as such. Neither is it about self-expression. I am only concerned with focusing on what I consider to be the fundamental themes.

This brings me back to my interest in cycles and series, and the necessity of working through the various dimensions, including the more shadowy visions of an idea. I'm accused of having a lyrical strain: something which presumably also doesn't fit with a radical stance. These are accusations which ignore the complexity, the concerns of critics with their own agenda.

I could argue that there are only two moments of significance. One is a moment of 'intimate touch', the other is 'sheer astonishment'. And very little between is of interest. They both meet at a point of silence.

Notes

1   This and the following quotation are taken from Keith Potter, 'James Dillon: currents of development', *Musical Times*, vol. 131, no. 1767 (May 1990), p. 259.

2   In his paper delivered to the Roehampton conference: see Chapter 1 in this volume.

3   See the composer's comments in interview with Richard Toop, in 'Four Facets of "The New Complexity" ', *Contact*, no. 32 (Spring 1988), pp. 4–50.

4   Dillon has in mind the composers La Monte Young, Terry Riley and Steve Reich.

5   The European Organization for Nuclear Research. The current website for this institution declares that 'CERN explores what matter is made of, and what forces hold it together'.

6   D'Arcy Wentworth Thompson, *On Growth and Form* (Cambridge: Cambridge University Press, 1961, abridged edition).

7   Dillon's list of composers here includes Hugues Dufourt, Gerard Grisey, Tristan Murail and Horatiu Radulescu.

8   See André Malraux, *The Metamorphosis of the Gods*, trans. Stuart Gilbert (London: Secker and Warburg, 1960).

9   Rainer Maria Rilke, *Letters on Cézanne*, trans. Joel Agee (London: Jonathan Cape, 1988).

10 The following quotations are taken from Whittall, Chapter 1 in this volume.

Chapter 10
An Interview with Edwin Roxburgh

Caroline Potter

CP: I'd like to start by asking about your studies, in particular about the time you spent with Nadia Boulanger.

ER: I studied with her for two summers in Fontainebleau [the Conservatoire Américain], and in Paris for several months. Certainly, she was no ordinary composition teacher! She was also a marvellous performer – a splendid organist – and I remember her performances of Brahms two-piano works with Dinu Lipatti, where you wouldn't know which pianist was Lipatti and which was Boulanger. And of course there was the monumental work she did on Monteverdi in the 1920s and 1930s, recording many of his works for the first time, with piano accompaniment of course, but that was the fashion in those days.

Keeping in mind that the major part of her life related to the first half of the twentieth century, I think her teaching methods were very much based on her absolute knowledge of Stravinsky, of everything he wrote. That, added to the fact that she was a very cultured woman who, for instance, would quote Shakespeare and Valéry during lessons, made her a fascinating teacher. I went to her as a 'mature student' in the sense that I had had a very thorough training at the Royal College of Music [RCM] with Herbert Howells, and after studying with her I went to Dallapiccola, about which she was very happy. When I came to her, I was more accomplished technically than those students who came to her at an earlier stage in their studies. The first thing I had to do for her was write a fugue, and she realized I could do that – otherwise, I would have had to go through her very rigorous training in harmony, counterpoint, and so on, but we got on to Stravinsky right away, which was nice.

CP: Did this involve analysing his works?

ER: Not employing any analytical method, because in those days analysis was a separate subject at the Conservatoire, and anyone who wanted to study analysis went to Messiaen. So really, it was just a question of her tearing my pieces apart!

CP: So where did Stravinsky come into this?

ER: Oh, pretty well every observation was related to Stravinsky. For instance, rhythmic characteristics – if you were going to write a pastiche, she would show how Stravinsky also committed the same sin, but the way he actually elaborated the music to such an extent moved the piece to a level above pastiche. At one point, I expressed my lack of ... understanding, I think, about the neoclassical phase – I couldn't see how anything 'neo' could be productive, and she got quite

5   Edwin Roxburgh

abrasive about that, actually. Similarly, Boulez would defend Stravinsky, not because of any positive liking of that period, but explaining the political and sociological position in the 1920s and 1930s which generated it. But it hasn't changed my mind, and I remember Dallapiccola describing this period as twenty years of dishonesty'! Interestingly, Boulanger saw a link between Stravinsky's *Movements* and Boulez's Second Piano Sonata, which was, of course, written at a very early stage in Boulez's career. She very much respected Boulez and understood him.

CP: Do you think there's something of a French flavour to some of your works? I'm thinking particularly of your flute music – the textures and sonorities in *Dreamtime* (1994) for flute and string orchestra, for instance.

ER: I'm happy to hear you say that! Debussy and Ravel have always been very close to my heart, and one reason why I went to study with Boulanger was my love of French music. Not only Debussy and Ravel interest me; earlier composers like Couperin and Rameau, and even earlier ones like Claude le Jeune – the rhythmic complexities of his chansons. So yes, I think I would accept that.

CP: Certain pieces of yours of the 1960s and 1970s feature space-time notation and new notational devices. Like many other composers, you seem to have rejected most of these devices in your most recent music.

ER: I think that whatever style, whatever idiom, which is thrown up by the conditions of the period you're living through, you have to take notice of it. I've been happy to absorb these 'vibrations', but not to be labelled with anything. I can't think of any composer, in truth, who accepts this kind of categorization. I hate this sort of 'specialist' characteristic anyway – contemporary music specialists, early music addicts, whatever. Especially where conducting is concerned, I *cannot* understand the age of specialization. I do not understand a conductor who prides himself on his expertise in Brahms or Beethoven and never touches Messiaen and Boulez. My reaction to this is related to my own early musical education, which I tried to make as broad as possible – at Cambridge, my special subject was Renaissance music. I really loved these composers, especially their counterpoint, which brings us on to Schoenberg.

So I don't really understand composers who want to identify themselves with a specific style. I would say, for instance, that John Adams is a perfectly good composer – but why does he limit himself to minimalism? Steve Reich hasn't moved on from his early style, and I find that boring. One should find a new grammar for the piece one is writing, or at least a development in the vocabulary. Beethoven did this consciously all the time.

As far as my 1970s pieces are concerned, certainly I did a few pieces which were graphically inspired. But I think that was an exploration, and really in line with my belief that composition is an adventure of discovery as much as invention. You make discoveries about your own material in writing a piece – that's part of the joy of composing. Where I would part company with graphic notation would be where composers just shoved some notes in boxes in a casual way. But where Boulez is concerned, especially in pieces like the third 'Improvisation sur Mallarmé' in *Pli selon pli*, I think he had magnificent ideas – the idea that a piece really *does* sound the same each time, but with incidental differences. But of course, the problem he had with that – I actually played it with him, when I played with the BBC Symphony Orchestra – is that, in the end, he had to write a definitive version, which is sad. Not so much because it didn't work as a concept, but because there wasn't sufficient time for the performers to go through the process required to learn the notation. I was very interested in this totally and utterly calculated improvisation (mobiles within mobiles) – *not* an improvisation which discounts the structure of the work. Like many composers, I went through this situation and have come out the other side, and I find myself in a situation where I can't really be identified with any common pursuit related to it.

CP: I was wondering whether, as an oboist and conductor, you find it difficult to 'let go' of pieces you have performed, whether you find it easy to be open to other interpretations.

ER: I have mixed experiences with that. I am full of admiration for marvellous performers like [the flautist] Michael Cox, who premiered my *Flute music with an accompaniment* (1986) – that is a quotation from Browning, by the way, not a comment on the accompanist! At the RCM, I have had marvellous performances conducted by Christopher Adey and Neil Thomson. And Peter O'Hagan, who of course commissioned my Piano Sonata (1993) and Six Studies (1980) – I feel very privileged to have worked with artists who are prepared to take the risk of taking on a piece of mine.

Coming to the negative side of this, I get a bit irritated by people who give as a reason not to perform my pieces 'because they're too difficult'. If anyone looks at a concerto or solo piano work by Rachmaninov or Scriabin, for example, how long do they take to learn those pieces? They are *extremely* difficult! The performers I've described and others have taken infinite trouble to find out why the virtuosity I've put into the pieces is needed. I also remember when Boulez came here [the RCM] last year, and a member of the audience asked him how he felt when other people conducted his pieces, and he replied: 'It's like lending someone your car!' I thought that was the perfect answer! Occasionally, my 'car' has been wrecked badly, especially the premiere of my 1977 Prom commission.

CP: That was *Montage* - it was performed again at the RCM in celebration of your sixtieth birthday.

ER: Yes. Christopher Adey did a wonderful performance with the Symphony Orchestra. It's a piece which is not necessarily difficult to play for the orchestra, but it's complex, and the textures are difficult to put together. One has to recognize how the seams join, because I don't see form in traditional terms at all. It rather reminds me of when Robert Saxton asked Takemitsu a question about the structure of one of his pieces, and Takemitsu's reply was: 'you open the cage, and the bird flies free to the skies ...'! I suppose that was evading the issue rather, but there's something of that in my approach to form, because the structure of a piece inevitably arises from the material, and not as a kind of, er ...

CP: Preset mould?

ER: Exactly. I even worry a little about Schoenberg in this context, although as you know, I profoundly admire his music. In something like the Wind Quintet, which is the first work demonstrating the absolute application of the 12-note theories, he's still using forms such as the rondo and sonata form, and with only one transposition of the row [sings it]. It's a very pompous work – the density of the scoring typical of Schoenberg, I suppose – but I do think that the structure of the whole piece, especially of the last movement, really doesn't carry the material as well as it could do, because you feel the old-fashioned 'reprise' characteristic really doesn't suit the material.

So, obviously when I'm thinking about a piece I get ideas for what it's going to be about, but the material itself develops slowly. Sometimes I actually start in the middle of a piece, because I want to have a feeling of direction *towards* the denouement or whatever it might be that the piece is about, so that I can see where it goes to and where it will go from. There has to be a nucleus somewhere in the piece. But it's not a hard and fast rule – I really take the direction my nose takes me in establishing how the piece is going to work, and gradually a framework builds up. I would never fully anticipate the structure of a piece before I get the material organized; I make dozens of sketches of the material first. The structure emerges gradually, not through a preset pattern of events. Nothing that can be Schenkerized too easily! I've never understood, incidentally, why Schenker's method has been applied to contemporary music, to the post-tonal era.

CP: I wanted to know to what extent your music is tailored for specific performers? I'm thinking especially of those works written for amateur performers.

ER: The broad issue about that is that one of the reasons why I admire Monteverdi is because he did write 'ars antica' and 'ars nuova', and he was able to adapt his style to the medium and to amateur singers. I think what I notice today is that fewer and fewer composers are conversant with the technical characteristics of music of the past. A 'real' composer ought to be able to write a piece in the style of Palestrina, Beethoven, Schubert or Bach, and recognize that the characteristics of the language are part of their heritage, part of their own vocabulary and grammar, and that their own compositions should arise from a thorough understanding of that. There is an obvious analogy with Picasso, whose classical paintings of his early days were absolutely meticulous in traditional techniques. And to be able to finish his life doing that incredible series of single-line drawings – the dove, for example – says everything about the very great artist that he was. He couldn't have done that without his training – it's the difference between being simplistic and being simple, which is a great difference.

So my thoughts about that, as far as my own music is concerned ... yes, I do consider the conditions under which the performance will take place. For instance, last year [2000] I was asked to compose a piece for the Sefton Youth Wind Orchestra in Liverpool, about which I was very enthusiastic. The Head of Music of the district, Geoff Read, used to be a clarinet student at the RCM, in the 1970s, and he's doing wonderful work up there. But he wasn't satisfied with so much of the repertoire that the wind band were playing, and he approached me for that reason – because I don't write traditional music, and he was very persuasive as to why he wanted me to write a new piece. So I took great pleasure in accepting the conditions – I had a list of all the young performers' examination grades, information about their capabilities, which one was very strong, and so on and I had that list in front of me all the time when I was composing. I felt writing for them was a very important issue, and I wrote a piece which wasn't patronizing towards them, but was within their technical capabilities, with one or two little glitches – but I felt it was important for me to challenge them a little bit as well. Even if every single detail wasn't there, they were enthusiastic and I was tremendously pleased with the performance. I'm very happy with the piece, although it's not in the same style as *Montage* or *Saturn* (1982), big pieces in which I used more progressive styles. So, yes, I do adapt – another example would be a piece I wrote for Tim Salter's Ionian Singers, *Pianto* (1985) – I used Italian words for that, Gatti's very touching hermetic poetry, and I attached a sort of modal concept to that. Diatonicism is one thing, and I still think it's possible to write a piece in C major, but you have to be a damn good composer to do it! It's a very saturated medium – there's bound to be a saturation point in any style. And my approach to the diversity we all see at the end of the past century is that we should be celebrating it – we should be able to write in different styles (not simply attaching ourselves to a particular idiom all the time) as indeed Bach and Beethoven did. I'm absolutely at ease adapting stylistic characteristics, as long as I'm in control of them, not writing pastiche. Some people, I think, might criticize my music occasionally because stylistic characteristics are mixed in one piece, and I'll accept that as criticism. It doesn't worry me too much, as long as I feel that the material itself is consistent within its structure. If there was a lack of stylistic cohesion, then I would be worried about that, but I don't sense that. But on the other hand, I'm very happy to hear such criticism to make sure that I take care that doesn't develop.

CP: I'd like you to talk about *Galileo*, which was first performed in 2000.

ER: That was a very complicated project because, essentially, it was a millennium commission and therefore it had to have a subject that seemed appropriate. I didn't particularly care about the millennium celebrations, but on the other hand, it's a subject that's appropriate to the commission and so I entered into the spirit, and chose a subject that I felt compelled by. I wanted very much to celebrate the marriage of science and music in the twentieth century – the way in which this has been manifested in the twentieth century is, of course, through the use of technology and the extended techniques which have arisen as a result. So I thought Galileo would be a good representation of this, because he was a physicist - and his father was a composer, so there's a connection there! In that amazing age of scientific and artistic revolution, Galileo was a very important focus. And he was a great character anyway, and I wanted to represent him in the first movement. The literature on Galileo's period is full of references to the discovery of the heliocentric theory and the acceptance of it, for instance in Shakespeare, whose text I used. And also the physicist Bruno, who was burned at the stake for proclaiming Copernicus' theories, and of course Galileo was criticized too, but he was a pretty shrewd man and managed to stay alive! So there's a vast amount of literature which I drew on in the first movement, and also used my own words. Here, I also used a baritone soloist to represent the figure of Galileo, so I could represent him as a strong character.

A variety of styles come into my choices sometimes. I had to consider, first of all, that there was very little rehearsal time – and in the end, there was even less than I had anticipated. Therefore, although the music was very much my own vocabulary, my own technique and my own style – my essential style, put it that way ... I felt the second movement needed to represent that, in spite of the technology available in the twentieth century, the history of the century, with two world wars, the conflicts in Korea, Kosovo, and so on needed to be reflected on. I feel that the younger generation has got a very clear perception of what my generation has been responsible for – it's ghastly. So I wrote a lament for the victims of conflict, and so that's a white-note piece, but with electronic colouring.

CP: And how about the involvement of children in the piece?

ER: Yes, I was very serious about that – I just thought that was one complication too many in the context of the programme. I felt that the concert of the childrens' GCSE compositions prior to the concert worked very well, and the idea of using Galileo as a subject was part of their educational programme – in other words, they had a history lesson, they learned something about astrophysics, they learned something about space in the twentieth century, and we ran a pilot programme in the Planetarium, which was very successful. They also worked with Michael Oliva with music technology – we had a wonderful day at the Warehouse and got a lot of fun out of that. Michael was surrounded by wide-eyed kids, all wanting to know how it worked, and he was very good at telling them. So that aspect was very good, but I think that the tableaux we had in the performance [composed by the children], in the context that we had to experience it, was possibly an element too many. I'd imagined it in a way that really wasn't achievable in the time we had, in spite of the excellent work by the animateurs, Avril and David Sutton-Anderson. Of course, the educational programme was one of those hoops we had to jump through in order to get funding from the Arts Council – and if I accept such terms, I want to make a creative endeavour out of it, which I tried to do. For the performance, the lack of rehearsal was a problem, and also the limitations of the technology in the Royal Festival Hall, where we had only two speakers! Jonathan Harvey had his *Mothers shall not cry* (2000) premiered at the Proms, and he had, I think, 12 speaker systems and bags of rehearsal time to get it right. So I felt robbed in a way by the circumstances, but I did feel it was a worthwhile creative endeavour.

CP: I'm interested that you mention Jonathan Harvey, because you seem to have much in common with him – for instance, your interests in the cosmos and in spirituality.

ER: Yes – but he's more of a mystic than I am. I'm not a religious character at all, even though I was brought up as a chorister in the Anglican Cathedral [in Liverpool]. I have the literary culture in my bones and I love it, but I'm not a practising Christian at all. But, leaving aside the denominational aspect of that, yes, spirituality is a very important part of my life. And I've always been interested in astronomy, and always tried to keep a very broad perspective on the aspects of my own existence.

CP: Finally, I'd like to ask about your work environment at the Royal College of Music. Is there any conflict between the essentially 'conserving' function of a conservatory, and the needs of the composer?

ER: Certainly, any institution is going to be conservat*ive* and, in some places, there is not sufficient recognition of the special needs of contemporary music, in terms of the exploration of new techniques, and adequate rehearsal time. Also, performers have special problems when approaching new music, as they have to come to grips with the style of a composer, which may be unfamiliar to them. But the enthusiasm and commitment of the students at the RCM can be marvellous for the composer – you can see the sense of achievement they feel when they've mastered a new piece. We set a very high priority on the performance of student compositions and the debate which accompanies this lively function is far from conservative.

Chapter 11

A Conversation with Sebastian Forbes

Ateş Orga

AO: Listening to your *Sonata-Rondo* for piano [1996], I'm conscious that its ending might remind some listeners of Stravinsky's *Les noces*.

SF: I think one is always aware that if you have a texture with, or involving, a very strong character, people are bound to suddenly think of other works which do a similar thing. I don't think I was guided too much by the Stravinsky, but the texture was what I wanted – then you think, well actually Stravinsky did something like this. But there's no similarity beyond that. People sometimes make connections between one piece and another which are invalid. I'm reminded of seeing Birtwistle's new opera, *The Last Supper*, with the twelve apostles coming back 2000 years later. They crept on to the stage in such deep thought that it reminded me not so much of excited apostles as prisoners from Beethoven's *Fidelio* or Janáček's *From the House of the Dead*. That's an obvious example of a totally irrelevant connection. Maybe the Stravinsky link with my *Sonata-Rondo* is equally irrelevant. Maybe it's just the sound of bells ringing and timelessness I wanted to create which Stravinsky also tried in *Les noces*. But that's as far as it goes. The chords are different.

AO: Looking at the *beginning*, a Messiaenic sense of rhythm, repetition and strategically placed rests comes across.

SF: The rests are deliberately half value. I've been fascinated with this idea ever since I got to know Messiaen's music in student days at Cambridge in the early 1960s. Messiaen himself said he was a rhythmitician first and foremost. He thought his contribution to rhythm enormous, which of course is true. What I've got from Messiaen, in my own way, I hope, is the idea of creating fantastic rhythmic energy completely separated from neoclassical groupings of rhythmic units into meters and pulse. I don't want regularity of pulse, but rhythmic energy is important – and rhythmic energy without groupings of notes into a pulse was one of Messiaen's biggest contributions. In the opening of *Sonata-Rondo*, though, I certainly wasn't thinking directly of Messiaen because these ideas have been part of my style for decades now, sometimes done with metrical exactness, sometimes, as in the Fourth String Quartet [1996][1] or the *accelerandos* of *Sonata-Rondo*, with apparent freedom.

AO: Yet still with a *sense* of beat ...

SF: Yes, but not a regular one. If you tried to dance to *Sonata-Rondo* you wouldn't do so to a regular old-fashioned metre, you'd be creating designs.

6   Sebastian Forbes

AO: Is there a larger regularity of beat across the whole?

SF: Not in this piece. Sometimes I'm obsessed with how many bars per section – and that happens in the Fifth Quartet [2000], where I wanted a gentle, understated concentration towards the end of the first movement. The last section is like the first, but brief and almost disappearing before you've realized it. How I did this was a case of exactness quite typical for me. I thought, let's have 18 bars for the first section, and then shorten each of the following successively by a bar. That'll give us a tenth at nine bars, exactly half length. This allowed me the telescopic focusing I needed for that moment. Sometimes these things are very, very carefully measured. In *Sonata-Rondo* they aren't, they're deliberately approximate. The big section at the beginning gets shorter and shorter on its reappearances. The second section, which is tiny, gets bigger and bigger, dominating by the end. I liken this to a 'cross-fade' – something big gets smaller, something small gets bigger. Inter-locking is another way to describe the process. You're aware of the smaller unit expanding, you're less aware of the bigger one contracting.

AO: The sonorities of one or two of your chordal blocks remind one of Copland. The piano Copland of the early Variations, the serial *Fantasy*.

SF: Again, that's accidental. I admire the Variations, although I was not conscious of them when I was writing this piece. Certainly in Copland – in both his more complicated works (the Piano Sonata, Variations) where he pursues particular configurations and intervals; and his more open-hearted pieces (the classic Copland, shall we say, of the early 1940s: the 'core' Third Symphony, *Appalachian Spring*) where his fingerprints are expressed in the simplest, most grandly generous way – one is aware that he was obsessed with certain interval patterns dominating his thought. Not so much a springboard for me, however, as Elliott Carter and *his* obsession with certain intervals, ideas and instruments.

Composing is full of doubts all the time. You think you're doing the same thing again and again. Yet some composers are actually proud of their obsessions. You have to be. If one is obsessed by certain formulations, a style, evolved genuinely, is going to gain by that. It's a matter of development, not repetition. Copland was a case in point. Beethoven, too, obviously. Particular sounds, certain concepts argued through, were their obsession. We are, of course, talking about music, *instrumental* music, that expresses itself in absolute terms, not dramatic music that refers to something outside itself.

AO: How do you explain a style 'evolved genuinely'?

SF: Creating anything places the artist into a whole series of uncertainties. Sometimes one's greatest creation is almost finished and you think, 'Is this rubbish or does it rise to something?' When I completed *Sonata-Rondo*, my immediate feeling was, 'It'll do for now but I'll rewrite some passages eventually'. In fact I didn't, not a single note was altered. But I wasn't sure of certain sections. Only looking at the music a week later did I find myself thinking, 'I'm not going to change this. That's it, that's staying'.[2] The sense of self-doubt is constantly there. It's got to be with any creative artist, I think. You're questioning yourself all the time. Is what you are doing valid? We all go through this agony of trying to construct something. You spend ages working something out. Then you think, 'Well, actually, that section is not dissimilar to one I worked out in another piece'. The very fact you've gone through your problem and worked it out only serves to reinforce the obsessiveness of how one composes. Some things come and go, of course. A particular idea isn't necessarily the same obsession years later – but the development of obsessive thinking is part of being a creative artist. Genuineness is accepting that certain concepts are going to dominate your thinking. In the end you'd be wrong to apologize for them. An awful lot of the devices, the schemes one goes through, leave little or no impression on the public – many of whom would probably simply recognize a piece as not having these schemes if they weren't there. There's a difference between perceiving, as a listener, that there is a solid structure, and the more detailed perception of knowing what that structure actually is and how it operates. Now, that understanding is not given to the ordinary listener or music admirer, and doesn't need to be. Maybe a conductor has it; sometimes the performer ... there are different levels of approach.

AO: And of course analysts, whatever the variety, can find out what composers don't state.

SF: Sometimes. And occasionally analysts will find things a composer may have forgotten about or was hardly aware of – and which the listener can't even hear. Is this valid? I remember some years ago a postgraduate student of mine claiming that it was a bit like the fourth-leg-of-a-table syndrome. If you have a straight table and you can see three of its legs, you know full well, without looking underneath, that there has to be a fourth because the whole thing is standing up. If it wasn't there, it would fall down. Likewise there are certain devices in music, certain aspects, which the composer has devised which no listener may be able to perceive as such, but if such devices were not present the piece would be weaker and collapse, even if you can't hear them. That's the table syndrome. Much of the enormous, behind-the-scenes technical apparatus a composer goes through will *not* be perceptible by even the keenest ears – and that's true not just of twentieth-century music but of a Beethoven, a Brahms, a Bach, whoever ...

AO: ... the agonizing of Beethoven's sketchbooks ...

SF: ... Yes, quite. A composer's severest critic is himself. Sometimes one struggles for a morning to get a passage, a line of music right and you come up with something that looks desperately simple. A great deal of thought has to be expended before you arrive at a solution. Beethoven's sketchbooks are the obvious example of that. All composers sketch. Beethoven's are only unusual in that he put so much down in sketch form. Webern's sketchbooks, as preserved, are not sketchbooks at all, they're desperately neat. An awful lot of thinking must have gone on in his head.

AO: But wasn't that true also of Beethoven? Maybe he clings to a germinal seed (say, the *Appassionata*'s F minor/G flat dynamic[3]), yet the relationships between sketch and solution can be so distanced, the intervening ground so undocumented, that to attribute decisions of rejection or acceptance to anything but mental processes *en route*, to those clarifications of doubt that come in sleep, would seem perverse.

SF: That certainly has a parallel with Webern. The Quartet for Saxophone is a wonderful example. Several attempts, different rhythms and notations for the first couple of bars. Then, once he's got the first bar right, the piece flows. The agonising thing of *exactly* how it should be expressed must have been torturous at the time. With both composers one can imagine a lot of sketching, a lot of questioning, going on in the mind which didn't find its way onto paper. Nobody's sketchbook tells us why some things were kept because they were apparently 'right', why others were abandoned because they were supposedly 'wrong'. And they tell us nothing of those occasions when, as it were, you 'see' the totality of a piece before you. The idea of *seeing* a piece of time is nonsense but one can have visions, as Stravinsky had dreams. My Fifth Quartet came to me in a flash. There it was. And that's happened before. It happens to many people.[4]

AO: Visually, the way you've tabulated the structure of *Sonata-Rondo* suggests an arch-form – although one that, in the Bach/Beethoven tradition, isn't proportionately exact.

SF: If the sections were the same length, it would be an arch, but they're unequal – though some of the events are exactly symmetrical, placed around the centre.

AO: As a young man you became interested in passacaglia, sectional processes, even before sonata principle. Passacaglia, from Bach to Brahms, Purcell to Webern, matters to you.

SF: True enough. This goes back to my earliest work in the late 1950s. And a crucial influence then, as later, was the slow movement of Rawsthorne's First Piano Concerto, where an eight-bar passacaglia basis modulates on each recurrence: not only repetition, therefore, but also progression. Many examples of this can be found in my music of the 1960s, such as the slow movement of the Piano Trio [1964], the orchestral Chaconne of 1967 (later revised as *Sinfonia 1*), and the Finale of the First String Quartet of 1969. The challenge to Baroque passacaglia writers – Bach and Purcell being the greatest, and Monteverdi of course (he began it really, as a form) – was to *offset* something stubborn, immovable and repetitive with expressive melody of contradictory character. Monteverdi's *Lamento della Ninfa* is the classic example of a species of descending scale endlessly repeated enhanced by just such melody. *Dido's Lament* nearly a hundred years later is another. The strictness of an immovable element counteracted by the struggle towards greater expressivity of the melody that surrounds it: in a way, that's a very simple example of how much music is created. Back to theme and variations again. You have a constant and a variable, you offset the two. When it comes to repetition, a characteristic of my 'mosaic structures' is that an idea may reappear in a different context. If you have more than two themes, half a dozen even, you can imagine 'Theme 1' reappearing not just in front of, say, 'Theme 2' but between 'Theme 5' and another version of 'Theme 3'. It's a different context. It makes 'Theme 1' *feel* different. It intensifies, I think, what Keller was getting at, that when you hear something again, it's in the light of what else you've experienced or what surrounds it, that's it's not a first encounter, that it may be varied or summarized in some way. Repeating things in different contexts is a random calling to mind, in a sense ...

AO: You talk about the wedge-structure of *Sonata-Rondo*, its 'cross-fade' construction. Looking at the sections, at how the music spreads up the registers, starting low, the texture intensifying to a high point, one senses a foreshortening process at work.

SF: Yes. A momentary telescoping of rhythms ...

AO: ... again, Beethovenian ...

SF: ... in the sense that Beethoven will drive a point to a climax by having a four-bar phrase followed by a three-bar one and then a two and so on. I don't think I got my idea from this but I'm aware of it because I admire him for it. It's all bound up with the notion that music can rarely stay put. If a piece is moving up or down, getting faster or slower, or moving towards a certain point, it preserves a sense of direction, even in the short term. A passage that starts with quavers and ends in demisemiquavers is a way of gradually accelerating to a point. Notationally, since my Organ Sonata [1968], I've found this a more conducive method of working, a more controllable means of telescoping events than putting simply *accel* or a beam splitting into three, because I'm controlling the rate of *accelerando* (or *decelerando* for that matter[5]), how fast or slow, precisely. In any situation I can create a direction towards a point by a series of note-values that are not even, but accelerating or changing in a measured way.

AO: Would you consider the concept of sections accelerating or decelerating in a controlled way a soundprint of yours, as it was occasionally of Brahms – the decelerating coda of the G minor Rhapsody from Op. 79 for instance? Inherently 'loose', *sul tasto* instructions like 'ritardando' are not often met in your music.

SF: Yes I think it might be a 'soundprint', in the sense that it happens in a lot of my music – though it's difficult to extend to whole textures. In the Fourth Quartet, for instance, one hopes that within sections individual players can enjoy a certain freedom in playing their own parts, *providing* they're clear when things should be synchronized again – often at a crucial chord which means something structurally. Within a texture you have 'fantasia bits' that look and feel random but are in fact very tightly controlled.

AO: These 'fantasia bits' allowing the performer an illusion of freedom, Lutoslawski's 'controlled aleatoricism' reapplied – *Sonata-Rondo* doesn't seem to encourage such licence ...

SF: I'm more in control here, and quite deliberately. It's a tighter structure, every element happening a certain number of times – transformations following statements. Nothing is left to chance. Obviously there's freedom in an *accelerando* from quavers to demisemiquavers in the course of a phrase because you can't strictly measure it in terms of how many crotchets it lasts. But, that said, there's very little freedom for the performer in *Sonata-Rondo*. Intentionally so.

AO: There're not many bar-lines in *Sonata-Rondo* – but there's no escaping the metronome indications, sometimes in very close juxtaposition. How critical are these markings?

SF: Ideally, very critical indeed. Not so much in terms of proportional relationships but in so far as a new idea carries with it its own texture, 'key' centre, and rhythmic identity. Rhythmic identity is crucial here. It reminds me of a piece I wrote years ago, the Partita for clarinet, cello and piano [1966], in (rare for a 'partita') one movement. I justified the label 'partita' because every idea in the piece had its own rhythmic identity – subordinated to the same overall pulse so I could juxtapose them yet keep the same beat going. What I learnt from this procedure is that a new idea should carry with it not only melody or harmony but also a rhythmic profile. In *Sonata-Rondo*, different metronome marks reinforce the identity of different ideas.

AO: The opening is marked crotchet = 96. If a pianist played at, say, crotchet = 100, would this concern you?

SF: Not necessarily, because an exact pulse here is not quite so crucial as those occasions where one writes music causing streams of semiquavers where an exact speed is more critical. It's hard enough for the pianist to be thinking in terms of crotchet = 96 as a guide because you can't reduce the music to a whole series of crotchets: the first demisemiquaver, for instance, is a rest between two semiquavers. That negates the notion that things can be subordinated to a crotchet pulse.

AO: You use the word 'obsession' a lot ... What were your obsessions in writing *Sonata-Rondo*?

SF: The main one, I think, was the 'cross-fade' idea. A search for form is funda-mental to the creative artist. If you have an idea, it has to be expressed, so how do you express it? Music is expressed in time, and form is related to the drama unfolding in time. That's true as much of sonata-form as opera. So how does one express a structure? One of my obsessions, nagging the mind now and again, is what I call 'mosaic form' – where different ideas can *reappear* in different contexts. Simply settling for a situation where you state this idea, that idea, and then go back to the first one rarely satisfies. There are subtle ways of *arranging* ideas so that they have different relationships, and that's one of the things I've tried to pursue in this piece. I didn't start with the thought that there must be eight themes – there happen to be eight – I just had the idea that the opening expression of frustration should dissipate as it reappears, with the secondary theme starting as a gesture then becoming bigger and bigger. That gives elements needing to be balanced. First, a structure that stands as an architectural framework; secondly, alongside – which seems a paradox – a sense of narrative. I think there's a feeling nowadays that music has lost its narrative. True, certainly, of the postmodernists. (Some would claim that postmodernism doesn't exist: it does of course – 'skin-deep mysticism', one critic's summary, where hardly anything happens. Post-modernism is supposed to 'move'. Well it doesn't move *me*, it infuriates.) I believe a sense of narrative, however unpopular in some circles as an ingredient of instrumental music, must always be strongly present. Narrative is forward motion through a piece, architecture the more static stability factor. The interac-tion between the two is important. A theme may reappear. What do you do with it? Repeat it, vary it? Summarize it, contrast it? Make it bigger, smaller, higher, lower? That's the directional point. It gives forward momentum. Narrative sense, architectural framework. Balancing those two factors is a strong feature of *Sonata-Rondo*.

AO: You talk of transforming a theme on repetition. Schoenberg would argue that for the listener when a theme comes back it's changed anyway, psychologically, in so far as you've heard it before and your perception is going to be different in the light of events experienced between statements; that, therefore, there is no such thing as a 'repeat'. Would you ever bring back an idea, a theme, *exactly* in the form in which it was originally presented?

SF: Occasionally yes, although I remember once being criticized for this in my First Quartet [1969], when Thea Musgrave said of a passage, 'Look, you must watch your form because this bit comes back exactly the same as before'. My answer, which she wasn't ready for, was that given the nature of the piece, this had to be. That was the whole idea, that at a certain point a block formation should recur exactly. Unusually in a sense because mostly it *would* come back in a different form, even if occupying the same number of bars ...

AO: ... the ornamenting, changing refrains of the Mozart A minor Rondo syndrome ...

SF: ... in the Fifth Quartet nothing is repeated exactly. Hans Keller was right I think – in the context of a Haydn minuet-and-trio, the *da capo* of the minuet *feels* different because of the experience of the trio. The 'repeat' of a classical sonata exposition, for much the same reason ...

AO: ... justifying implementation ... Is this need for material change on repetition the classical development process 200 years down the line?

SF: If one is going to repeat exactly there has to be a good reason for doing so. I tend to allude rather than repeat. One of the ways to allude is to have something before upside down or backwards or both. Sometimes, however, things are so constructed in my music that the retrograde inversion is the same as the beginning anyway. *Whole* passages of my music will do this now and again. It's an obsession which I have to say is part of my style – balanced, I hope, by a demand for certain tonal progression as well.

AO: You frequently use the word 'tonality'. In *Sonata-Rondo* you have whole sequences you define as 'tonal areas'. How do you explain a 'tonal area'?

SF: Something literally central. A note that's the exact centre of a symmetrical chord – the third of an augmented triad, for instance, a chord that on inversion remains the same thing. A liking as well for what Graham George over 30 years ago identified as 'interlocking tonality'[6] – where a secondary key takes over. The D major of Mahler's Fifth Symphony for instance. It's not there at the start. It creeps in. It dominates the last movement. Meanwhile, the first key, C sharp minor, has died. Now Mahler was the first to apply this concept as a symphonist. The Fourth begins in G major. E is there, its dominant, B, present in the very first line of music ...

AO: ... likewise at the climax of the slow movement, pivoting the music from G to E ...

SF: ... certainly, though it's not confirmed until the finale, which eventually establishes E major as 'home'. 'Interlocking tonality' is our 'cross-fade' idea if you like. The first key dies, the second key is there, it becomes omnipresent by the end. Was Mahler, though, so blazingly brand new in this technique? Certainly, he was extraordinary for ending works in keys he did not begin in. And symphonically, yes, the procedure was new.[7] Yet it's always happened in opera and oratorio. All he did was to apply it to symphonies. It's a dramatic concept applied to a non-dramatic medium. This 'interlocking' of tonalities is interesting, the sense of tidy progression, too. We use the words 'tonality', 'tonal centre', 'pitch centre', even 'pitch class centre', often very loosely, intending to convey a generalized definition. But the sense of *progression* operating within each is very important. If I have a carol to set in five verses, it would be natural, to me, to set each verse a minor third apart [C–A–F#–Eb–C; C–Eb–Gb–A–C] because then you would have a progression ensuring that the fifth verse was in the same key as the first – this has been the case for me since the 1960s.

AO: ... the principle behind the descending, alternating minor/major third keys of Beethoven's Op. 34 Variations, or the ascending major third relationships of Schubert's *Wanderer* Fantasy, Brahms's First Symphony ...

SF: ... Indeed, look what happens in my *Reflections* for chamber organ [1998] – six reflections on a tiny Rawsthorne theme.[8] It made sense to have 1, 3 and 5 inverted – giving a structure finishing with the theme the right way up. You don't necessarily perceive this as a listener – but, unquestionably, it guided me. 'Tonality', my music ... ? 'Tonality' in the traditionally referential understanding[9] is really the wrong word. The nearest it gets to being the 'right' one is probably in something like my first set of Evening Canticles written for Christ Church, Oxford, in 1980. In the Magnificat, diatonic keys are more evident, the top voices rising tone by tone until we get back to B-flat again, twice over, the bottom voices falling tone by tone at half the speed. This gives a lot of bitonal relationships, but the sense of movement and progression is there all the time, a preconceived plan through which the music is moving, constantly going on to the next event in the story.

AO: Examining the 'tonal areas' of *Sonata-Rondo*, each, irrespective of register, reinforces a single pitch. Certain sections you could almost reduce to 'fantasies on one note'. Are your 'tonal areas' concerned with individual pitch emphasis?

SF: In some ways yes. Individual notes and their degrees of prominence are certainly an important ingredient of the tonal configuration.

AO: But without the 'old world' pull of tones and semitones ...

SF: I've never accepted 'atonal' as a concept. Schoenberg as you know preferred 'pantonal': he didn't like 'atonal' as a term because, strictly speaking, it means 'without notes'. I think there's an area *between* what's now called 'common practice tonality' – an abstraction with which, I have to say, I'm not wholly in agreement – and that which isn't. After all, 'common practice tonality' comes and goes in Debussy – extraordinarily. In my piece I didn't want to make it *so* obvious. Again, there's a balancing factor involved. To what extent do you want to make a scheme evident enough to be logical, but not *so* evident that everyone knows what's going to happen next. Sometimes the note around which a section is constructed is deliberately obscured. It's there, structurally; it doesn't have to be thrust on the listener.

AO: 'Tonal area', then, or 'pitch area'?

SF: 'Pitch area' would be better. Sometimes these pitches are a very strong

book

ingredient of certain configurations of notes that have their own tensions within them. The *exact* notes chosen (and played) are crucial.

AO: I remember you saying to me some years ago that 'too many people persist in thinking of an idea as a simple melody [...] might not an idea after all be a texture with a certain kind of melodic cell around it'[10]...

SF: ... yes, that's true ...

AO: ... 'I don't think in terms of melodic identity,' you argued, 'as something exclusively separate.'

SF: A colleague, the late Hans Heimler,[11] once remarked about my music years ago – and he was absolutely right – that, essentially, it's harmonically conceived, the melodies arising out of the available notes comprising the harmonic core of an idea. The rhythmic texture, of course, is essential to the equation, but it's the harmonic element that's crucial.

AO: Which places you firmly in the Beethoven/Brahms tradition.

SF: I'm not ashamed of that. I think Brahms remains my favourite composer. And you know my enthusiasm for Beethoven and his chamber music. It's enduring.

AO: In *Sonata-Rondo* you're preoccupied with eight 'thematic images' – less 'themes' in the common understanding (though you called them that) than many-dimensioned 'identities' or 'personalities': theme with you means something frequently different from what it might represent for someone else.

SF: I remember in one programme note actually putting 'theme' into inverted commas. In some of my 'mosaic form' music – the Cello Fantasy [1974], *Sonata for 8* [1978] – if you have a number of 'themes', for want of a better word, coming in various arrangements or reappearing at unexpected junctures, they can interact like personalities in a conversation or characters on a stage. Sometimes it's good to play around with these things in the sense that you leave one theme deliberately unaltered – one thinks of those famous perfect fifths in Strauss's *Ein Heldenleben*: come what may, two critics ever unmoved. That's a lovely idea because in a 'mosaic' context one theme may refuse to develop, rather like a personality in a crowded room refusing to say anything, or alter his opinion. Whole themes can dramatically transform themselves because of conversational interaction. That's enlarging the idea of 'theme' as a purely musical concept to one of 'character'. A theme to me is a character, a personality, with the capacity to change direction in the course of a conversation – or not; with the potential to dominate – or accept defeat ...

AO: ... bringing Janáček, another favourite composer of yours, to mind, how events run their course in the Sinfonietta, for instance ...

SF: *Yes!* Strong contrasts presented without apology is an obvious factor in Janáček that appeals. Sometimes the expected cadential tidying-up of an idea doesn't happen: if you're looking for a compendium of interrupted cadences there's nothing better than Janáček (well, perhaps Wagner). When you think the music is going to settle, it shoots off, seeding the next bit. The wonderful thing to me in Janáček is how a tiny germ of an idea can give rise to so many divergent themes. He gets lots of personalities – and aligning them thematically, you can see how they all answer to a certain shape. That doesn't quite apply to my music, but the contrasts of these different personalities, the sense of a lively conversation between different minds taking place – that's exciting.

AO: What decided the title '*Sonata-Rondo*'? 'Rondo' because of the recurrence of ideas? 'Sonata' because ... ?

SF: 'Rondo' because of the expectation that an idea will return. 'Sonata' because, in common with my other instrumental sonatas, it expresses itself in purely musical, abstract terms and argues musical points. I'm not thinking of 'sonata *form*' in any sense at all. Rather, I use the word 'sonata' in its loosest possible sense, not just in terms of a Stravinskyian 'sounding' but to indicate a piece of music without external reference, concerned with concepts of substance, continuity and structure. And narrative: a classical sonata, after all, is about narrative as much as drama. I wanted to debate these issues.

AO: 'Narrative', 'opera', 'drama', 'conversational interaction', 'personality' – the leitmotifs of your language. You're an artist who's always thought symphonically, in the abstract. Cherishing the mainstream repertory from Beethoven through Brahms to Bartók, you speak of the string quartet as the 'highest form of musical interplay'. Your father's time with the Aeolian Quartet was the sound and background of your childhood. What about opera, does the genre interest you, as it has done your contemporaries?

SF: Yes – but more in instrumental terms than writing for the theatre. I'm not drawn naturally to the medium. Despite the fact that vocal music has been part of me since the cradle, despite having spent a lifetime singing in or conducting choirs – it's instruments that give me, compositionally, the note formations and ingredients I need to play around with – which don't lend themselves so easily to vocal delivery. Looking back I think some of my work for unaccompanied chorus is perhaps my least successful.[12] Instrumental music is where my strongest contribution may lie.

AO: You place logic before rhetoric, cohesive argument before heart-on-the-sleeve gesture – fashioning an expressive complex of powerful emotional chemistry. Your analytical perceptions and differences are those, urgently those, of a composer, a practical, practising musician, not a theorist. Physical circumstances, extra-musical events have never had much bearing on your work.

SF: It's important to know one's artistic personality.

Notes

1   Based on the choral cycle *This is England* (1981).
2   Accepting that detail can always change, Forbes places a high premium on *formal* decision, typically questioning the validity of those whom he perceives to lack it: Bruckner the symphonist, for example.

3   See Frohlich, M., *Beethoven's 'Appassionata' Sonata* (Oxford: Clarendon Press, 1991).

4   Recalling a meeting with Beethoven in 1823, J.R. Schulz, *The Harmonicon*, vol. 2 (1824), reported that he 'never writes one note down till he has formed a clear design [in his mind] for the whole piece'; of Chopin, Jeffrey Kallberg maintains, 'larger notions of structure and melody were likely shaped in his fingers *and mind*' (*Chopin at the Boundaries*, Cambridge, MA: Harvard University Press, 1996, our italics).

5   For a *locus classicus* of forelengthening procedure see the retransition of the first movement of Beethoven's E minor Piano Sonata, Op. 90, bars 132ff – semiquavers becoming quavers becoming crotchets becoming minims.

6   George, G., *Tonality and Musical Structure* (London: Faber & Faber, 1970); Robert Simpson, *Carl Nielsen: Symphonist 1865–1931* (London: Kahn and Averill 1952, rev. edn 1979), speaks of 'progressive tonality', 'evolving tonality', tonality as a 'dynamic view'; Robert Bailey (ed.), *Wagner: Prelude and Transfiguration from 'Tristan und Isolde'* (New York: W.W. Norton 1985), refers to 'directional tonality'.

7   Simpson, however, points out that the innovation of Mahler's Second Symphony was anticipated by Nielsen in his First (1891–92): 'possibly the first [such work] to end in a key other than that in which it started'.

8   This theme is from Alan Rawsthorne's *Madame Chrysenthème* (staged by Sadlers Wells Ballet at Covent Garden, 1955); it is heard at the start and close of the ballet and is scored just for unaccompanied, wordless mezzo-soprano.

Example 11.1   Alan Rawsthorne, *Madame Chrysenthème*, theme at start and close of ballet

9   Choron's *'tonalité moderne'* (1810).

10   Orga, A. 'Sebastian Forbes: a 50th Birthday Profile', *Musical Times*, vol. 132 (May–June 1991), pp. 234–7, 290–92.

11   Formerly Lecturer in Music at the University of Surrey; before the Second World War a student of Berg, Schenker and Weingartner in Vienna.

12   Contrast Christopher Mark's view that Forbes's 'music tends to be most character-istic when ... he is responding to specific poetic images' (*The New Grove*, rev. 2nd edn, London: Macmillan, 2000).

Index

Page references in *italics* relate to illustrations

accessibility of music, 34, 41–2
Adams, John, 143
Adès, Thomas, xvi–xvii, *4*, 6, 14–16, 22, 25
   Arcadiana, xv, 3, 5, 14–24
   Darkness visible, 15
   Lyric Suite, 25
Adey, Christopher, 143–4
Adlington, Robert, *author of Chapters 4 and 7*
Aeolian Quartet, 159
allusion, xv–xvii, 5–14, 25, 136–9, 156
amateur performers, 145
d'Arezzo, Guido, 41
art music, 33–6, 42
Arts Council, 34, 40, 43, 147
Arts Ministers, 40
atonal compositions, 157
avant-garde music, 32, 120

Babbitt, Milton, 63, 120
Bach, J.S., 5, 36, 39, 44, 103, 146, 153
   St John Passion, 103
Bainbridge, Simon: *Concertante and Moto Perpetuo*, xvi
Barthes, Roland, 6
Bartók, Béla, 6, 11, 103, 159
   String Quartet No. 2, 11–12, 139
BBC (British Broadcasting Corporation), 45
BBC Radio 3, 29
BBC Symphony Orchestra, 143
Beethoven, Ludwig van, xvi, 6–7, 36, 103, 143, 146, 151–3, 158–9
   Fidelio, 40
   Grosse Fuge, 61, 115–16
   Missa Solemnis, 85
   String Quartet, Op. 130, 22
   Variations, Op. 34, 157
Berg, Alban, 22, 39

Lulu, 103
Lyric Suite, 22
Violin Concerto, 5
Birtwistle, Harrison, 3, 11, 31, 111–17, *112*
   Carmen Arcadiae Mechanicae Perpetuum, 58
   Entr'actes and Sappho Fragments, 114
   Five Distances, 48, 111, 114
   Harrison's Clocks, 48
   The Last Supper, 111, 149
   The Mask of Orpheus, xviii
   Monody for Corpus Christi, 56
   Nine Movements for String Quartet, 47–61, 111
   Pulse Shadows, 47–8, 50, 113
   Refrains and Choruses, 48
   Secret Theatre, 113
   Slow Frieze, 49–51
   Todesfuge, xv
   Tragoedia, 114–15
   Verses for Ensembles, 58
Bloom, Harold, 5–6
Boethius, 45
Boulanger, Nadia, 141–2
Boulez, Pierre, 31, 33, 39, 45, 47, 64, 144
   Piano Sonata No. 2, 142
   Pli selon pli, 143
Brahms, Johannes, 103, 158–9
   Rhapsody in G minor, 154
   Symphony No. 1, 157
   Variations on a theme of Haydn, 103–4
Britten, Benjamin
   String Quartet No. 3, 22, 25
   A Time There Was, 22
   The Turn of the Screw, xvi
Browning, Robert, 46, 143
Brunel, I.K., 44
Bruno, Giordano, 146

Buddhism, 121–2, 129
Byrd, William, 103

Cage, John, 126
Carter, Elliott, 11, 151
    String Quartet No. 2, 49
Celan, Paul, 47–8, 59, 61, 115, 117
Chopin, Frédéric: Ballade No. 2, 5
Chua, Daniel, 7
Classic FM, 29, 35
climate change in British music, 29–30, 32,
    34
composers in schools, 41
Connolly, Justin, xvi
contemporary music, use of term, 30–31,
    34–5
Contemporary Music Network, 30, 41
Cook, Nicholas, 85
Copland, Aaron, 150–51
Couperin, François, 39, 142
Cowan, Rob, 39
Cox, Michael, 143
Crew, Beverley, 30–31
cross-fade construction, 87–9, 153, 155
Cruft, John, 40–41
Cummings, E.E., 45

Dallapiccola, Luigi, 141–2
Debussy, Claude, xvi, 64, 103, 114, 120,
    142, 157
Dillon, James, xvi–xvii, 6, 25, 131–40, *132*
    Del Cuarto Elemento, 131
    Nine Rivers, 11
    String Quartet No. 1, 7
    String Quartet No. 3, xv–xvi, 3, 6–7,
        12–16
    Überschreiten, 7
    Via Sacra, 135
    Violin Concerto, 131–9
Divine Comedy, 31
Dowland, John: "In darkness let me dwell",
    15
dumbing-down, 42, 45

education, musical, 41–6, 147
electronic music, 64, 73, 127, 132
Elgar, Edward, 5, 19
Eliot, T.S., 5, 71
elitism, 40, 137
English National Opera, 41, 71, 121
Evans, Peter, 85

Eyre, Richard, 41

folk elements in music, 136
Forbes, Sebastian, 149–59, *150*
    Evening Canticles, 157
    Partita for clarinet, cello and piano, 154
    Reflections for chamber organ, 157
    Sonata-Rondo, xvii, 86–104, 149–59
    String Quartet No. 1, 156
    String Quartet No. 4, 149, 154
    String Quartet No. 5, 152
    also author of Chapter 6
Fox, Clare, 42–3
frieze concept, 49–59, 115–16
fugue, 59–61, 115–16

Galileo project, xvi, 43–5, 146–7
Genghis Khan, 40
George, Graham, 85, 156
Gerhard, Roberto, 86, 105
Goodman, Lord, 40
graphic notation, 143
Grisey, Gérard, 76

Hall, Michael, 47–8, 51, 54, 115
Hamburger, Michael, 61, 115
harmonic element in music, 158
'harmony of the spheres', 44
Harvey, Jonathan, xvi–xvii, 63–83,
    119–29, *120*
    Advaya, 73–6, 82, 124
    Ashes Dance Back, 76
    Bhakti, 120
    Calling Across Time, 81–3
    Cello Concerto, 65, 121
    Inner Light, 122
    Inquest of Love, 71–2, 76, 121
    Mortuos plango, vivos voco, 76
    Mothers shall not cry, 78, 147, 128–9
    Percussion Concerto, 64–9, 125
    Ritual Melodies, 119–20
    Scena, 71, 76, 121
    Soleil Noir/Chitra, 77–80
    String Quartet No. 2, 126
    String Quartet No. 3, 65, 70, 76
    Valley of Aosta, 63
    Wheel of Emptiness, 126
    White as Jasmine, 128
Haydn, Josef, 33, 103
    String Quartet in C (Op. 54/2), 7
Heimler, Hans, 158

Hinrichsen Foundation, 40
Holloway, Robin, xvi
Holst, Gustav, 56
Howells, Herbert, 141
Hoyland, Vic, 25
    Bagatelles for string quartet, 25

influences, musical, 5, 25
information theory, 39
Ionian Singers, 145
L'Itinéraire, 64

Janacek, Leoš, 158–9
    Sinfonietta, 158
Jarvis, Robert, 43
le Jeune, Claude, 142
Johnson, Julian, xvi–xvii; *also author of
    Chapters 2, 5 and 8*
Joseph, Sir Keith, 41
Josquin Desprez, 33
Joyce, James, 133, 138

Keller, Hans, 63, 86, 153, 156
Kenyon, Nicholas, 32
Knussen, Oliver: *Ophelia Dances*, xvi

Lassus, Orlandus, 44
Lee, Jenny, 40
Lesh, Phil, 11
Lipatti, Dinu, 141
Liszt, Franz: *Années de Pèlerinage*, 22
Lloyd, Jonathan: *Three Dances*, xvi
Lloyd-Webber, Julian, 32
London Festival Orchestra, 43–4
London Planetarium, 43, 147

McCartney, Sir Paul, 42
MacGregor, Joanna, 31
MacMillan, Peter, 7
Mahler, Gustav, 33, 123, 156
Malraux, Andre, 138
Marsh, Roger, 25
Maus, Fred, 48
Maw, Nicholas, xvi
Maxwell Davies, Peter, xvii, 7
    Eight Songs for a Mad King, xvi
Mellor, David, 40
melodies, 120–21, 158
Meltdown Festival, 30
Messiaen, Olivier, 76, 119, 141, 149
microtones, 127

Milton, John, 44
minimalism, 45
modernism, 31, 33, 39, 73, 81
Monteverdi, Claudio, 141, 145
    Lamento della Ninfa, 153
    Vespers, 52, 117
Mozart, W.A., 5, 22, 39, 116
    Jupiter Symphony, 119
    Rondo in A minor, 156
Murail, Tristan, 76
Musgrave, Thea, 156

new notes (magazine), 30–32
Niedecker, Lorinne, 111

O'Hagan, Peter, 143–4
Oliva, Michael, 43, 147
open strings, 115
opera, 159; *see also* English National
    Opera
Orga, Ateş, *author of Chapter 11*

palindromes, musical, 103–4
Park Lane Group, 45
Pascal, Blaise, 44
passacaglia form, 153
peripatetic music teachers, 41
Picasso, Pablo, 145
pluralism in music, 31–4
Pople, Ross, 44
Porter, Andrew, 16
post-modernism, 155
Potter, Caroline, *author of Chapter 10*
Potter, Keith, *author of Chapter 9*
Pountney, David, 121
progressive tonality, 95, 104
pulse, 134–5
Purcell, Henry, xvi
    Dido's Lament, 153

Rachmaninov, Sergei, 144
Rameau, Jean Philippe, 142
Rattle, Simon, 39
Ravel, Maurice, 142
Rawsthorne, Alan, 104–105
    Piano Concerto No. 1, 104, 153
Read, Geoff, 145
Reich, Steve, 143
relativism, 32, 35
repetition, 155–6
rhythmic energy, 149
Rilke, Reiner Maria, 7, 138

Rimbaud, Arthur, 11
Rosengard Subotnik, Rose, 4
Rossini, Gioachino, 40
Roxburgh, Edwin, xvi–xvii, 141–8, *142*
    Dreamtime, 142
    Flute music with an accompaniment, 143
    Montage, 144
    Pianto, 145
    also author of Chapter 3
Royal College of Music, 141, 147–8
Royal Festival Hall, 147
Royal Opera, Covent Garden, 41
Rudkin, David, 121
rules, breaking of, 123

St John-Stevas, Norman, 40
Salter, Tim, 145
samsara, 129
Sanders, Elma, 49
Saxton, Robert, 144
Schlee, Alfred, 53
Schoenberg, Arnold, xv, 39, 143, 155, 157
    Chamber Symphony, 119
    Wind Quintet, 144
Schubert, Franz, xvi, 5, 22
    Tenth Symphony, 104
    Trout Quintet, 104–6
    Wanderer Fantasy, 157
Schumann, Robert, xvi
    Kreisleriana, 21
Scriabin, Alexander, 144
Second Viennese School, 39, 120
Sefton Youth Wind Orchestra, 145
self-allusion, xvii
serialism, 64
Shakespeare, William, 44
Shaw, Bernard, 45
sketchbooks of composers, 152
Society for the Promotion of New Music,
    30, 45
specialisation by musicians, 143
spectral tonality, 82
spectralism, 73–6, 127–8, 136
steady state concept, 3
Stein, Erwin, 63
Stephenson, Sir Denis, 41
Stockhausen, Karlheinz, 42, 114
    Stimmung, 136
Straus, Joseph, 5
Strauss, Richard: *Ein Heldenleben*, 158

Stravinsky, Igor, 33, 141–2, 152
    Les noces, 149
    Serenade in A, 5
    Symphonies of Wind Instruments, 22
style, musical, 138
subsidy, 39–40
Sutton-Anderson, Avril and David, 43, 147
symmetry, 89–95
'systems music', 135

Takemitsu, Toru, 144
Talbot, Joby, 31
tango form, 14
Taruskin, Richard, 5
Tavener, John, 3
Tchaikovsky, Pëtr Ilyich, 40
texture, 149
themes, concept of, 158
Thompson, D'Arcy, 135–6
Thomson, Neil, 143
timbre, 136–7
Tippett, Michael: *The Knot Garden*, xvi
tonality, 156–7; *see also* progressive tonality
Toop, Richard, 6, 8, 41
transcendence, 124
Turnage, Mark Anthony, 3
    Before Dark, xvi
Turner, J.M.W., 63–4

understanding of music, 85–6

Varèse, Edgar, 6–7

Wagner, Richard, 119, 158
    Die Meistersinger, 22
    Parsifal, 76
Walker, Sarah, 41
The Warehouse, 147
Webern, Anton, xv, xvii, 33, 39, 103
    Five Pieces for Orchestra, 71
    Quartet for Saxophone, 152
    Six Bagatelles for String Quartet, 65
Whittall, Arnold, xv–xvi, 51, 61, 81, 131,
    138–9; *also author of Chapter 1*
Wilde, Oscar, 45
Woolrich, John, 116

Zehetmair, Thomas, 131
Zemlinsky, Alexander von: *Lyric
    Symphony*, 22